Kings, Usurpers, and Concubines in the *Chronicles of the Kings of Man and the Isles*

"This work shines a critical light on a rather shadowy period of history. The historical heroes and villains of the Kingdom of Man and the Isles are characters worthy of any modern fantasy TV drama. Andrew McDonald's usual academic rigour untangles the reality from the myth, leaving an important reference work and a thoroughly readable story."

—Allison Fox, *Curator: Archaeology, Manx National Heritage*

"In *Kings, usurpers, and concubines*, R. Andrew McDonald turns a case-study of the thirteenth-century manuscript chronicling the hero-kings of Man and the Isles into a thoughtful, coherent, and convincing elucidation of what he pithily terms 'the deadly game of Manx thrones' from roughly 1079 to 1275. The book is equal parts scholarly and accessible—a difficult balance to achieve. This is a stimulating and highly-recommended read."

—Professor K.S. Whetter, *Acadia University*

"*Kings, usurpers, and concubines in the Chronicles of the Kings of Man and the Isles* is an important contribution to European and Atlantic history with its fresh examination of the Kingdom of Man and the Isles. Andrew McDonald's new reading of the source materials leads to an ambitious interpretation of the events from the kingdom's origins to its loss of independence. He gives particular attention to the fraught political manoeuvrings of the mid-thirteenth century as the rulers of the Isles attempted to maintain their independence in the face of plotting by the kings of Norway, England, and Scotland to add the island kingdom to their respective realms. McDonald's use of multiple methodologies combined with a close reading of the primary records illuminates the history of a significant, but neglected, region of Europe."

—Professor Benjamin Hudson, *Pennsylvania State University*

R. Andrew McDonald

Kings, Usurpers, and Concubines in the *Chronicles of the Kings of Man and the Isles*

palgrave
macmillan

R. Andrew McDonald
Department of History
Brock University
St Catharines, ON, Canada

ISBN 978-3-030-22025-9   ISBN 978-3-030-22026-6   (eBook)
https://doi.org/10.1007/978-3-030-22026-6

This Palgrave Pivot imprint is published by the registered company Springer Nature Switzerland AG.
The registered company address is: Gewerbestrasse 11, 6330 Cham, Switzerland

FOR JACQUELINE, EMMA, AND COLIN

PREFACE

The Isle of Man is a small but fertile island, approximately 572 km^2 in extent, situated in the middle of the northern Irish Sea basin, roughly equidistant from the surrounding lands of England, Scotland, and Ireland, all of which are visible from it under favourable conditions. In fact, it is said that from the summit of Snaefell, the highest peak on the Island (620 m), seven kingdoms are visible: Man, England, Scotland, Wales, Ireland, the sea, and heaven. There is more than a little truth in that saying, for although it may be difficult to believe today, 800 years ago, the Isle of Man lay at the heart of a transmarine kingdom that extended from the Calf of Man to the Island of Lewis in the Outer Hebrides: the Kingdom of Man and the Isles. For two centuries, from about 1079 to 1265, this far-flung maritime kingdom was ruled by first one and later two vigorous dynasties of sea kings who descended from the mysterious warlord Godred Crovan who conquered Man in 1079 and died on Islay in 1095.

The mid-thirteenth-century text known as the *Chronicles of the Kings of Man and the Isles*, compiled, in all probability, at Rushen Abbey in the Isle of Man, tells us most of what we know about these kings and their exploits. Although short, it is full of vivid (if brief) descriptions of rulers and other important figures, dramatic intrigues, plots, and rivalries worthy of "Game of Thrones," and tantalizing but often obscure glimpses into Manx and Hebridean society in this forgotten kingdom of the medieval British Isles. This little volume began life as a lecture entitled "Heroes and villains in the *Chronicles of the Kings of Man and the Isles*" presented at the Manx Museum in Douglas and kindly hosted by Manx National Heritage in December of 2015. This was originally intended as a brief and hopefully entertaining investigation of the Manx kings and their rivals as they appear in the *Chronicles*, highlighting some of its intriguing comments on rulers like Godred Crovan (who "so tamed the Scots that no one who built a ship or boat used more than three iron bolts"), his son Olaf Godredsson (d. 1153, praised as "devout and enthusiastic in matters of religion and … welcome both to God and men, except that he over-indulged in the domestic vice of kings"), or Magnus Olafsson (d. 1265, who was "received with grace and honour" and knighted by Henry III of England). Set in opposition to these hero-kings, the *Chronicles* denigrates rivals and challengers like Somerled of Argyll (d. 1164) and his descendants as "the cause of the break-up of the kingdom," while other dynastic rivals from within the Manx ruling kindred are also castigated as tyrants and usurpers. The text thus has the appearance of a dynastic chronicle designed to legitimize the status of the Manx kings: hence, the kings and usurpers of my title.

As work progressed, however, I found myself struck by the question of why women seemed to be particularly vilified by the compilers of the *Chronicles*. It seems noteworthy to me, for instance, that, although the female presence in the text seems marginal at best, at two separate places in the text the compiler explicitly blames women for disasters that afflicted the Kingdom of Man and the Isles. In the early twelfth century, the marriage of a daughter of King Olaf of Man (d. 1153) to Somerled of Argyll is said to have caused "the collapse of the entire Kingdom of the Isles." In the early thirteenth century the "wicked wish" of a (mysteriously) unnamed Queen of the Isles apparently re-ignited a titanic struggle for the kingship between the brothers Rognvald and Olaf Godredsson that culminated in the death of Rognvald in battle near Tynwald in 1229. The much-neglected female presence in the text, coupled with the prejudices of the compiler of the *Chronicles*, therefore provides the concubines of my title.

In an important study of noblewomen in Wales in the High Middle Ages (a period more or less contemporary with that addressed here), Susan M. Johns argues that, "placing women and gender at the heart of the analysis raises new questions about the construction of history."[1] In this work I wish to suggest, among other things, how placing women and gender alongside an analysis of the male heroes and villains of the *Chronicles of the Kings of Man and the Isles* serves to raise new questions concerning the dynamic interactions of gender, power, and historical writing and memorialization in the medieval Kingdoms of Man and the Isles, thereby providing new insights into the meaning and significance of the text that is our most important source of information on these forgotten kingdoms of the medieval British Isles.

St. Catharines, ON, Canada   R. Andrew McDonald

NOTE

1. S. M. Johns, *Gender Nation and Conquest in the High Middle Ages: Nest of Deheubarth* (Manchester, 2013), 229.

BIBLIOGRAPHY

Johns, S.M. 2013. *Gender, Nation and Conquest in the High Middle Ages: Nest of Deheubarth*. Manchester.

ACKNOWLEDGEMENTS

This study began life as a lecture presented at the Manx Museum in Douglas, Isle of Man, in December 2015, and I am very grateful to Manx National Heritage for sponsoring, organizing, and hosting the talk. I would also like to express my profound appreciation to Allison Fox of Manx National Heritage for organizing the lecture, for discussion of many points presented in the talk and the manuscript, and in general for many years of collegial assistance with my research. I am similarly grateful to Peter Davey and Philippa Tomlinson for their hospitality during my numerous visits to the Isle of Man, and for their willingness to share their insights into many aspects of the archaeology, landscape, and environment of the Island, and to Andrew Johnson at Manx National Heritage for his longstanding collegial assistance. Angus A. Somerville and Kevin S. Whetter offered many helpful suggestions on several drafts of the work, which would be much poorer without their kind advice and wisdom. I am also grateful to David Caldwell, Seán Duffy, Benjamin T. Hudson, Alan MacNiven, and Linzi Simpson for discussion of many facets of the medieval Kingdoms of Man and the Isles over the years and for continually challenging my thinking on the subject. These people bear no responsibility for the use I have made of their advice and any remaining infelicities are to be attributed to the author alone.

I must acknowledge the efforts of the Inter-Library Loans staff of the James A. Gibson Library at Brock University (Jan Milligan, Mary Little, Sue Sykes, and Oksana Voronina) for tolerating my many requests for research materials with stoicism and also for unfailingly procuring them for me. Many thanks are also due to Loris Gasparotto for his assistance with the maps and table for the book.

Students in my fourth-year seminar on sources of medieval history at Brock University have endured reading both the *Chronicles of the Kings of Man and the Isles* and early drafts of this work since 2015, and I am very grateful for their interest and enthusiasm and in particular for their questions and comments that have helped to improve this work.

At Palgrave Macmillan I am grateful to Emily Russell and Oliver Dyer for soliciting the manuscript and for expert editorial guidance throughout, and to their team for the professionalism with which they guided the book through production. I am also grateful to the anonymous reviewer of the manuscript for suggesting improvements.

Finally, on the domestic front, I am continually thankful for the complete and enthusiastic support that I have always received for my work from my wife, Jacqueline Buchanan, and our children, Emma and Colin. My children have grown up with the Manx sea kings but have never complained about having to share their father with them, and some of our happiest times as a family have been spent exploring the world of the sea kings together in the Isle of Man, England, Wales, Ireland, and Scotland. This book is for my family.

CONTENTS

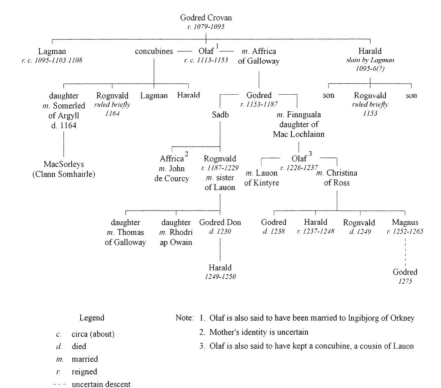

Godred Crovan
r. 1079-1095

Lagman *r. c. 1095-1103 1108*	concubines —— Olaf[1] —— *m.* Affrica *r. c. 1113-1153* of Galloway		Harald *slain by Lagman 1095-6(?)*

daughter
m. Somerled
of Argyll
d. 1164

Rognvald
*ruled briefly
1164*

Lagman   Harald

Godred
r. 1153-1187

Sadb

m. Finnguala
daughter of
Mac Lochlainn

son

Rognvald
*ruled briefly
1153*

son

MacSorleys
(Clann Somhairle)

Affrica[2]
m. John
de Courcy

Rognvald
r. 1187-1229
m. sister
of Lauon

Olaf[3]
r. 1226-1237
m. Lauon   *m.* Christina
of Kintyre   of Ross

daughter
m. Thomas
of Galloway

daughter
m. Rhodri
ap Owain

Godred Don
d. 1230

Godred
d. 1238

Harald
r. 1237-1248

Rognvald
d. 1249

Magnus
r. 1252-1265

Harald
1249-1250

Godred
1275

Legend

c.   circa (about)
d.   died
m. married
r.   reigned
- - -   uncertain descent

Note: 1. Olaf is also said to have been married to Ingibjorg of Orkney
2. Mother's identity is uncertain
3. Olaf is also said to have kept a concubine, a cousin of Lauon

Table 1   The sea kings descended from Godred Crovan, c. 1079–1275

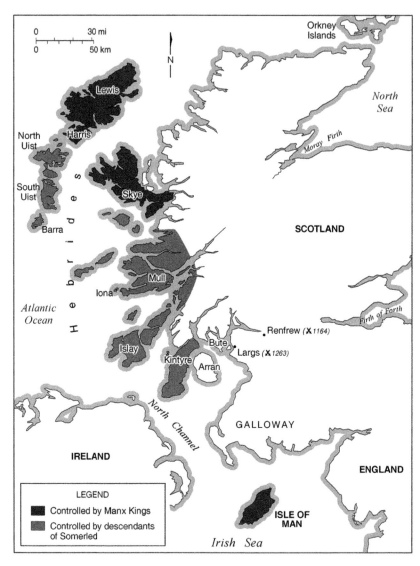

Map 1 The Kingdoms of Man and the Isles c. 1200

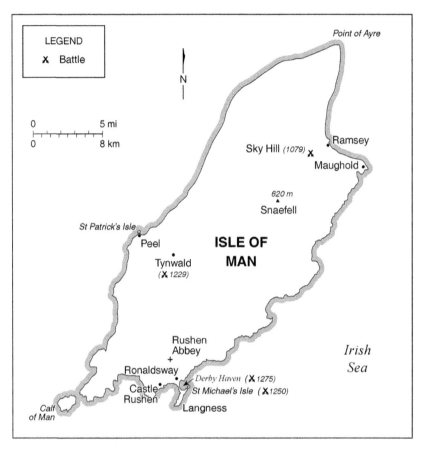

Map 2 The Isle of Man

CHAPTER 1

Introduction: A Medieval Manx Game of Thrones

Abstract The thirteenth-century text known as the *Chronicles of the Kings of Man and the Isles* represents the single most important historical text for the late Norse Kingdom of Man and the Isles from about 1066 to 1265. The focus of the *Chronicles* on the ruling dynasty of Man and the Isles and many dramatic, game-of-thrones style episodes relating to power-struggles within the dynasty presents an impressive array of heroes and villains for analysis. Examination of the representation of kings, usurpers, and other heroes and villains in the text, as well as of gender and power, provides a key to unlocking the significance of the text.

Keywords *Chronicles of the Kings of Man and the Isles* • Crovan dynasty • Sea kings • Kingdom of Man and the Isles • Power-struggles • Gender and power

Between the years 1248 and 1252 a deadly game of thrones played out in the Kingdom of Man and the Isles, a transmarine realm situated in Atlantic Britain and stretching from the Isle of Man in the south to Lewis in the Outer Hebrides. The catalyst for the crisis was the tragic drowning of King Harald of Man (r. 1237–1248), aged only about in his mid-twenties, along with his new bride, Cecilia, the daughter of the Norwegian king, and their entire retinue in a shipwreck in the treacherous waters off Sumburgh Head in Shetland in the autumn of 1248. Following the

© The Author(s) 2019
R. A. McDonald, *Kings, Usurpers, and Concubines in the* Chronicles of the Kings of Man and the Isles,
https://doi.org/10.1007/978-3-030-22026-6_1

tragedy, King Harald's brother, Reginald (Rognvald), succeeded him in the kingship, but events then proceeded from bad to worse, as Reginald was assassinated mere weeks into his reign, and a vicious struggle over the kingship raged down to the year 1252. The principal protagonists in the struggle were Reginald's brother and eventual successor, Magnus (d. 1265), famous as the last reigning member of the dynasty; Harald, the son of Godred Don, a grandson of the earlier Manx king Rognvald (d. 1229) and so a member of the royal kindred; and Ewen, son of Duncan (d.c. 1268), a descendant of the Hebridean chieftain Somerled, a kinsman of the Manx kings, and a major player Irish Sea and Hebridean politics from the 1240s to 1260s:

> In the year 1249 Reginald son of Olaf began reigning in Man on 6th May. On the 30th day of the same month…he was killed by the knight Ivar and his men in a meadow near the church of the Holy Trinity in Rushen to the south of the same church. He was buried in St. Mary's Church, Rushen… Then Harald, son of Godred Don, usurped the title and dignity of king in Man for himself and banished practically all the chieftains of King Harald, Olaf's son. In their place he introduced his own chieftains and nobles from exile…In the year 1250 Harald, son of Godred Don, summoned by a letter, went to the court of the lord king of Norway. The king was angry with him for presuming to seize a kingdom to which he had no right, and he detained him in Norway intending never again to let him return to the Sodor Isles. The same year Magnus, son of Olaf, and John [Ewen], son of Dougal [recte Duncan; see chapter four], with some Norwegians came to Man and landed at the port called Ronaldsway. John [Ewen] son of Dougal sent envoys to the people of Man, who said, "John, King of the Isles, orders you to do this and this." When the Manxmen heard John being called King of the Isles and not Magnus son of Olaf, they were very angry and refused to hear the envoys' words further.[1]

These passages are taken from the thirteenth-century text known as the *Chronicles of the Kings of Man and the Isles*, the single most important historical text for the late Norse Kingdom of Man and the Isles from the late eleventh to late thirteenth centuries. An important characteristic of the text is its focus upon the ruling dynasty of Man and the Isles, and, as these passages suggest, it is full of dramatic episodes relating to power-struggles in the kingdom that present an impressive array of both heroes and villains. Apart from the mysterious assassin Ivar about whom little is known, there is Harald, the son of Godred Don (the son of King

Rognvald Godredsson), demonized as an usurper; there is reason to think (see below) that Ivar was somehow associated with Harald and we might well wonder whether the assassination of Reginald and the usurpation of Harald were not in some manner connected. Then there is "John son of Dougal," properly Ewen son of Duncan (fl. 1248–1268), a member of a rival dynasty of sea kings that makes regular appearances in the *Chronicles*, and he appears in a similar guise as a would-be usurper. Set against these figures, the heroes of these passages are the brothers Harald (r. 1237–1248), Reginald (assassinated 1249), and Magnus (r. 1252–1265)—the sons of King Olaf Godredsson (r. 1226–1237), the "rightful" kings of Man and the Isles. Lest there is any doubt about the oppositional characterizations of these individuals as heroes and villains, a carefully positioned miracle story inserted into the text at this point reinforces the illegitimacy of Harald, the son of Godred Don, and demonstrates that God is on the side of the rightful line of kings represented by the drowned Harald and his brother Magnus (more on the miracle in Chaps. 5 and 6).

Mention of Medieval Manx hero-kings will inevitably call to mind Godred Crovan, the conqueror of the Isle of Man in 1079, the victor of the great battle at Sky Hill, and the founder of a dynasty of sea kings that held power in Man and the Hebrides for over a century and a half after his death in 1095. Famous in Manx legend as King Orry, he might have gone down in Manx history as Godred the Conqueror.[2] This study, however, is *not* about Godred Crovan as a hero of Manx history, although he will certainly have his place in the examination that follows. Its emphasis is, rather, upon Godred's descendants, the members of the dynasty that he established, both well behaved and poorly behaved, and the manner in which they are presented in the *Chronicles of the Kings of Man and the Isles* which tells us most of what we know about them.

This little book has two aims. First, it explores heroes and villains from the folios of the Manx chronicle. It will begin with some obvious heroes and obvious villains, and progress from there to some less obvious ones, with what will, I hope, turn out to be some rather surprising revelations. In the course of the investigation, however, we will encounter the problem of trying to understand exactly what the compiler of the *Chronicles* was hoping to accomplish by producing the work: in other words, as in any historical investigation, we have to consider *how* we know as well as *what* we know. In the final analysis, we will see that there is in fact a crucial link between the heroes and villains of the chronicle and the very nature of the text itself; as we shall see, the vilification of Harald son of Godred Don and Ewen son of Duncan in the passage cited above is far from accidental.

Before we embark on our investigation, a few quick comments on terminology and conventions utilized throughout. First, I use the terms "heroes" and "villains" loosely without any reference to classical, historical, philosophical, or literary-critical definitions, where the term "hero" in particular has a well-defined set of criteria. Nevertheless, some sort of descriptors is necessary. Since practically any terms will evoke at least some literary connotations, since the material in question is rather storied at times, and since the principal figures do fall clearly into categories of good and bad, "heroes" and "villains" seem the most appropriate way of describing the individuals at hand. Second, the principal text utilized throughout, the so-called *Chronicles of the Kings of Man and the Isles* (see further below) has been described in many different ways over the years. For the sake of convenience I will refer to it in shorthand as the *Chronicles*, or the Manx chronicle, or sometimes simply the chronicle. Unless otherwise noted, I always use and cite the most recent scholarly edition by George Broderick (1995), and I refer to folio rather than page numbers for the sake of a convenient concordance with this edition.[3]

Finally, a word on the forms I have used to render personal names. The complex linguistic situation in Man and the Isles in the period under consideration, where both Gaelic and Norse were spoken, and where Latin was the principal language of learning, means that a potentially bewildering array of forms may be, and has been, utilized for personal names by authors writing on the subject. Thus, for example, King Rǫgnvaldr of the Icelandic sagas was known in Gaelic as Raghnall, and, to further complicate matters, in Latin sources like the Manx chronicle he becomes Reginaldus. There is no accepted scholarly convention for rendering these names, and I will, therefore, for the sake of convenience, use anglicized forms—although I do so with the caveat that the underlying linguistic situation is far from clear. Where I cite passages from the Manx chronicle I have allowed names to stand in the Latinized form utilized by George Broderick, with the result that Rognvald appears as Reginald.[4]

Before we delve into the heroes and villains of the text, we must begin with a brief discussion of the nature of the document itself.

NOTES

1. *Cronica Regum Mannie & Insularum. Chronicles of the Kings of Man and the Isles BL Cotton Julius A vii*, ed. G. Broderick (2nd ed., Douglas, 1995; repr. 1996; 1st ed., 1979), f. 48r–48v [hereafter *CRMI*].
2. J. Feltham, *A Tour Through the Island of Mann, in 1797 and 1798; Comprising Sketches of Its Ancient and Modern History, Constitution, Laws, Commerce, Agriculture, Fishery & c.* (Bath, 1798), 9; the sobriquet does not seem to have stuck. Godred's career is analysed in S. Duffy, "Man and the Irish Sea World in the Eleventh Century," in S. Duffy and H. Mytum (eds.), *New History of the Isle of Man, Volume III: The Medieval Period 1000–1406* (Liverpool, 2015), 9–26 and in B.T. Hudson, *Viking Pirates and Christian Princes: Dynasty, Religion, and Empire in the North Atlantic* (Oxford, 2005), 170–185.
3. Broderick, *CRMI*, provides the Latin text with a facing page English translation. This is a user-friendly edition that is still in print. Broderick also published, with Brian Stowell, a translation of the *Chronicles* in English and in Manx Gaelic, *Chronicle of the Kings of Mann and the Isles. Recortys Reeaghyn Vannin as ny h Ellanyn* (Edinburgh, 1973). Before Broderick's edition and translation appeared, the most important version was that of P.A. Munch, *Chronica Regum Manniae et Insularum. The Chronicle of Man and the Sudreys*, with an English translation and historical notes (Christiana [Oslo], 1860); this was revised by Rev. Goss and published by the Manx Society (Douglas, 1874). A rare facsimile of the extant manuscript is *The Chronicle of Man and the Isles: A facsimile of the Manuscript Codex Julius A. vii in the British Museum*, with introduction, translation, and bibliographic notes by W. Cubbon (Douglas, 1924); it is probably rendered redundant by the digital images available at http://www.bl.uk/manuscripts/FullDisplay. aspx?ref=Cotton_MS_julius_a_vii
4. There is a convenient concordance of names in J. Copeland, "Names Concordance," in S. Duffy and H. Mytum (eds.), *New History of the Isle of Man, Volume III: The Medieval Period 1000–1406* (Liverpool, 2015), viii–ix. On the complex linguistic situation and some of the problems associated with it see M. Gelling, "Norse and Gaelic in Medieval Man: The Place-Name Evidence," in P. Davey (ed.), *Man and Environment in the Isle of Man*, vol. ii, 2 vols. (Oxford, 1978), 251–264; but compare B.R.S. Megaw, "Norseman and Native in the Kingdom of the Isles: A Re-assessment of the Manx Evidence," in Davey (ed.), *Man and Environment in the Isle of Man*, vol. ii, 265–314; see also R.L. Thomson, "Language in Man: Prehistory to Literacy," in Duffy and H. Mytum (eds.), *New History of the Isle of Man III*, 241–256. I am grateful to my colleague Angus A. Somerville for sharing his vast store of linguistic wisdom and advice.

BIBLIOGRAPHY

Chronica Regum Manniae et Insularum. The Chronicle of Man and the Sudreys, with an English translation and historical notes by P.A. Munch. 1860. Christiana [Oslo].

Chronica Regum Manniae et Insularum. The Chronicle of Man and the Sudreys, with an English translation and historical notes by P.A. Munch. 1874. Revised by Rev. Goss. Douglas.

The Chronicle of Man and the Isles: A Facsimile of the Manuscript Codex Julius A. VII in the British Museum, with introduction, translation, and bibliographic notes by W. Cubbon. 1924. Douglas.

Chronicle of the Kings of Mann and the Isles. Recortys Reeaghyn Vannin as ny h Ellanyn. 1973. Edited and translated by G. Broderick and B. Stowell. Edinburgh.

Copeland, J. 2015. Names concordance. In *New History of the Isle of Man, Volume III: The Medieval Period 1000–1406*, ed. S. Duffy and H. Mytum, viii–viix. Liverpool.

Cronica Regum Mannie & Insularum. Chronicles of the Kings of Man and the Isles BL Cotton Julius A vii. 1995. Edited by G. Broderick, 2nd ed. Douglas; repr. 1996; 1st ed., 1979.

Duffy, S. 2015. Man and the Irish Sea World in the Eleventh Century. In *New History of the Isle of Man, Volume III: The Medieval Period 1000–1406*, ed. S. Duffy and H. Mytum, 9–26. Liverpool.

Feltham, J. 1798. *A Tour Through the Island of Mann, in 1797 and 1798; Comprising Sketches of Its Ancient and Modern History, Constitution, Laws, Commerce, Agriculture, Fishery & c.* Bath.

Gelling, M. 1978. Norse and Gaelic in Medieval Man: The Place-Name Evidence. In *Man and Environment in the Isle of Man*, ed. P. Davey, vol. ii, 2 vols., 251–264. Oxford.

Hudson, B.T. 2005. *Viking Pirates and Christian Princes: Dynasty, Religion, and Empire in the North Atlantic*. Oxford.

Megaw, B.R.S. 1978. Norseman and Native in the Kingdom of the Isles: A Re-assessment of the Manx Evidence. In *Man and Environment in the Isle of Man*, ed. P. Davey, vol. ii, 2 vols., 265–314. Oxford.

Thomson, R.L. 2015. Language in Man: Prehistory to Literacy. In *New History of the Isle of Man, Volume III: The Medieval Period 1000–1406*, ed. S. Duffy and H. Mytum, 241–256. Liverpool.

WEBSITE

British Library: http://www.bl.uk/manuscripts/FullDisplay.aspx?ref=Cotton_MS_julius_a_vii

CHAPTER 2

The *Chronicles of the Kings of Man and the Isles*

Abstract The *Chronicles of the Kings of Man and the Isles* is a thirteenth-century collaborative work compiled by several anonymous authors, most likely at Rushen Abbey in the Isle of Man, and based upon a variety of sources, that serves as our main source for the history of the medieval Kingdom of Man and the Isles between the eleventh and early fourteenth centuries. It is not, however, an easy text to use, and must be sifted carefully to determine the value of the evidence that it provides.

Keywords *Chronicles of the Kings of Man and the Isles* • Medieval chronicles • Cistercian chronicling • Rushen Abbey • Source criticism

Among the texts contained within the manuscript British Library Cotton Julius A VII is a relatively short medieval Latin text known by the title *Chronicles of the Kings of Man and the Isles* after its opening rubric, which reads, *Incipiunt cronica regum mannie & insularum & episcoporum & quorundam regum anglie, scotie, norwegie*: "Here begin the Chronicles of the Kings of Man and the Isles and of the bishops, and of some of the kings of England, Scotland (and) Norway." Commonly known as the "Manx chronicle" or the "Chronicle of Man," and less commonly as "the Rushen chronicle" after its most likely place of composition, we do not, in fact, know how the text was referred to at the time of its compilation; the title *Chronicles of the Kings of Man* was apparently first used to describe it

© The Author(s) 2019

R. A. McDonald, *Kings, Usurpers, and Concubines in the* Chronicles of the Kings of Man and the Isles,
https://doi.org/10.1007/978-3-030-22026-6_2

only in the late sixteenth century.[1] Whatever we call it (and I use the terms
Chronicles, Manx Chronicle, and Chronicle of Man interchangeably
throughout), this is perhaps the single most important document in medieval Manx history as well as one of the most significant in Hebridean history: not only is it the earliest surviving piece of indigenous historical
documentation from the Isle of Man (excluding the remarkable corpus of
early medieval carved stone memorials with inscriptions found in the
Island[2]), but it also provides much of what we know about of the period
between about 1079 and 1300 in the Hebrides, the Isle of Man, and the
Irish Sea. The story that it tells is made all the more remarkable by virtue
of the fact that, so far as is known, this is the only surviving copy of the
manuscript in existence (although a later copy from this exemplar also
survives). Little wonder that it is regarded as a "national treasure" in the
Isle of Man,[3] and its return to the Island nation in 2007 and again from
November 2012 to March 2013 as part of a special exhibition at the Manx
Museum on "The Forgotten Kingdom? The Kingdom of Man and the
Isles 1000–1300" was greeted with considerable excitement. In fact, the
Chronicles have become something of a focus for modern Manx national-
ism, and calls have been made for the manuscript to be permanently dis-
played in the Isle of Man.[4]

The *Chronicles* provide a terse, factual, year-by-year account of significant historical events in the Isle of Man, the Hebrides (the islands off the
west coast of Scotland), and the rest of Britain from the year 1000 (actually 1016) to the final entry in the year 1316. From the year 1047 (cor-
rectly 1066) the *Chronicles* provide unique information relating to the Isle
of Man, its Norse-Gaelic rulers, and their connections with England,
Scotland, Ireland, the Hebrides, and Norway as well as the history of the
church and religious leaders in Man and the Islands. The text of the
Chronicles, which occupies folios 31r to 50r,[5] is followed by a list of the
bishops of the Isles that runs down into the fourteenth century (folios 50v
to 52r), and these are in turn followed by another document known as the
Limites or *Abbeyland Bounds*, a detailed survey of monastic lands in the
Isle of Man (folios 53r to 54v). The numbering of the folios was not contemporary with the production of the text, but since the most recent edition of the text maintains this numbering, for the sake of convenience I
will refer to folio numbers when making reference to the *Chronicles*.

Like most medieval chronicles, the text is anonymous and represents
the work of several unknown scribes. The text fills about 40 leaves, and
each leaf contains about 26 lines of text with about 9–10 words per line.

Five different scribes, identifiable by their distinct handwriting, contributed to it. A single scribe wrote the majority of the text up to the year 1257 and was also probably responsible for some of the interesting drawings of abbeys and crosses in the margins of the leaves, while four more scribes subsequently added additional material down to the final entry for the year 1316.[6] These same scribes also compiled the list of bishops contemporaneously with their chronicle entries. The fact that most of the text up until the year 1257 was written by a single scribe, as well as the nature of the handwriting, which is characteristic of the second half of the thirteenth century, suggests that the *Chronicles* were begun at this time, although some authorities prefer a slightly later date, in the early 1260s, for the composition of the text. Moreover, the fact that the entry for the year 1257 describes the (re-)dedication of the Church of St. Mary at Rushen in the Isle of Man—evidently a significant and grand event, since both Richard, Bishop of Sodor (d. 1275) and the King of Man and the Isles, Magnus Olafsson (r. 1252–1265), were on hand for it—has led to the further deduction that the *Chronicles* were probably commissioned for this occasion (possibly by the king) and were likely composed at Rushen Abbey itself, perhaps even by a Manx monk. The entry reads: "In the year 1257 St. Mary's Church at Rushen was dedicated by the venerable father and Master Richard, Bishop of Sodor, in the fifth year of his pontificate and in the presence of Lord Magnus King of Man and the Isles in the fifth year of his reign."[7]

These conclusions concerning the provenance of the *Chronicles* are buttressed by its interest in events pertaining to the abbey, which is mentioned on several occasions within the text, as well as its knowledge of Manx affairs, a knowledge that is probably best explained by its composition on the Island itself.[8] It is possible that the *Chronicles* might have been composed at Furness Abbey in Cumbria, the mother house from which Rushen Abbey was founded in 1134, but most scholars have tended to prefer a Manx origin for the text. Small clues within the text support this contention. It is difficult, for example, to see why a non-Manx chronicler would choose to refer to King Magnus as returning "home" to Man from Norway in 1254 and from England in 1256, and it is also noteworthy that the chronicler mentions the beauty of the island in the context of the visit of King Magnus Barelegs in 1098, something that might be expected of a native of Man.[9] The author also seems to demonstrate fairly detailed knowledge of the Manx landscape and environment, which similarly points towards a native identity for the compiler: he knows, for instance, about the harbour at Ramsey, the "sloping brow of the mountain called Sky Hill," and the practice of keeping watch over the coasts which is credited with repelling an attack in 1172, to mention only a few such details.[10]

The Manx chronicle is by no means unique, of course: about 25 such texts were produced in Cistercian houses in the British Isles in this period.[11] They were created and maintained for a variety of purposes. Although they are usually regarded as historical records, they also had liturgical, computistical, and administrative functions: the role of these chronicles as historical records was complex and multifaceted, as "Cistercian annalistic writing arguably served many complementary purposes."[12] These ranged from the promotion of corporate identity of the broader Cistercian community to the recording of local events, and chronicles could also serve as dynastic histories.[13] In fact, the three-cornered relationship between the Manx kings, Rushen Abbey, and the Manx chronicle is, as we shall see, crucial to understanding the nature of the text. Indeed, Bernadette Williams, in her contribution to the medieval volume of the *New History of the Isle of Man* dealing with the *Chronicles*, goes so far as to suggest that the intense focus of the text upon the dynasty of the Manx kings means that it is "not a monastic chronicle within the normal meaning of the term," although this is certainly open to debate.[14]

The fact that the *Chronicles* was composed at the time of *some* of the events that it records (or within living memory of them) and that it provides unique information on the period, gives it unparalleled significance as an historical source. But the fact that a large part of it was composed retrospectively—that is, by a scribe in the mid-thirteenth century looking *back* over nearly two centuries' worth of history—raises important questions about not only where the compiler or compilers may have obtained their information, but also about the general reliability of the Chronicles as an authority for the historical events that it describes. How trustworthy is the *Chronicles of the Kings of Man and the Isles* as an historical source?

There is nothing inherently unusual about the retrospective aspect of the chronicle: the narrative of many of the Cistercian chronicles produced in the medieval British Isles begins in the distant past rather than with the events of their creators' own times, and the Creation, the Incarnation, and the Norman Conquest of England were all used as starting-points by various chronicles.[15] Nevertheless, there are certainly a number of challenges associated with the use of the *Chronicles* as an historical source. Among students of Manx, Hebridean, and Irish Sea history the Manx chronicle is notorious for its chronological problems, which manifest themselves in several different ways. Events can be misdated; the events of a number of years can be compressed into a single entry; and the sequence of events can be out of order. The problem of misdating is especially pronounced in the entries up to the 1150s. Godred Crovan's conquest of the Isle of Man, for instance, is placed by the *Chronicles* in 1056 rather than 1079, and his death is placed in 1075 rather than 1095. Another example is found in the *Chronicles'* dating of the accession of Godred's son, Olaf, to the kingship. This is said to have occurred in the year 1102, but we are then told that he reigned for 40 years and died in 1153.[16] Since the date of his death is correct (as demonstrated in the subsequent entry of the *Chronicles*), either the length of his reign or the date of his accession to the kingship must be in error. Current scholarship seems to favour accepting a reign length of 40 years and therefore corrects the date of his accession to 1113, but older scholarship was more inclined to accept the Chronicle's date of his accession and adjust his reign length accordingly. The matter remains uncertain, and the chronology and events of the period between 1095 and c. 1113 in Man and the Isles remains extremely murky and problematic at best.[17]

Fortunately, the *Chronicles* improves significantly in its chronology from the second half of the twelfth century. The errors in the earlier parts of the text may be due to scribal error or to a lack of source material, either written or otherwise, on the part of the compiler—or both. In fact, in the first entry in the list of bishops appended to the *Chronicles*, penned by the same scribe who wrote the main body of the text to 1257, the compiler comments upon the lack of surviving information for the time before Bishop Hrolf, the first bishop named, observing that, "we are totally ignorant of what/which bishops there were before him [Hrolf, the first bishop named], because we have found no record, nor have we learned anything certain from the tradition of our elders."[18] This interesting observation highlights some of the challenges faced by the compiler of the chronicles in the 1250s, and it has been remarked that the compilers of the *Chronicles* may have known even less about the origins and early history of the Kingdom of Man and the Isles than do modern scholars—a sobering thought given the nature of the gaps in our knowledge of this subject in the early twenty-first century.[19]

The greater degree of accuracy exhibited by later entries suggests more reliable information as the events covered by the chronicle move closer to the time of composition. That some of this information was even obtained at first hand can be seen in the *Chronicles'* account of events that occurred in the period 1249–1250, when, at the conclusion of an anecdote concerning a chieftain named Donald, the chronicler states, "This we have written just as we learned it from his own mouth [i.e. from Donald]."[20] It is also noteworthy that entries towards the end of the text are generally longer and more detailed than earlier ones. This is because these events are close to the date the manuscript was recorded, and many probably occurred within living memory of the scribe. Thus, not all parts of the text can be considered to be equally useful to the historian.

Reference to the first-hand information obtained from the chieftain Donald mentioned by the chronicler raises important questions about where the compilers obtained their information. As noted, by the middle of the thirteenth century, at least, the compilers of the text claimed to be able to draw upon eyewitness testimony from participants in some of the events being described, and this certainly comprises one significant type of source material. Another related type of information that could have been utilized has also been referred to above, namely, what the compiler of the chronicles refers to as "the tradition of our elders," or oral tradition. This probably underlies the *Chronicles'* statement of King Olaf that, "Many anecdotes about him worthy of being remembered could be told," and it has been demonstrated how oral testimony formed what has been called a "staple source" for medieval hagiographical texts, for example.[21] It is possible that a similar tradition underlay the short verse preserved under the year 1275, attributed to a "certain rhymster." Whether these verses already existed in their own right, or whether they were composed specifically to be inserted into the text, is not known, and either is possible (see more on this below).[22] Finally, it is not beyond the bounds of possibility that the scribe of the *Chronicles* himself had been an eyewitness to some of the events he describes. Some of the entries, such as that describing the final showdown between the brothers Olaf and Rognvald at Tynwald in February of 1229, for example, contain such a wealth of detail that it is tempting to suppose that the scribe himself had witnessed the events.

The compilers of the text also seem to have had access to different types of written records and materials. Medieval monasteries, particularly those in the Cistercian tradition, served as repositories of documents and centres of manuscript production.[23] A variety of sources have been identified as having been utilized in the compilation of the *Chronicles* by scholars who have considered the matter. These included chronicles such as the thirteenth-century Scottish *Chronicle of Melrose* (compiled at the Cistercian abbey of Melrose in the Scottish borders) for a good deal of information relating to events outside the Isle of Man down to 1193, and from the northern English *Chronicle of Lanercost* for material between the 1230s and 1270s; while it is thought unlikely (because of the date of its production) that *Lanercost* itself was used by the compilers of the Manx chronicle, is it possible that common source material was utilized by both?[24] Finally, since there is so much detail about events in England in the early part of the *Chronicles*, before unique Manx information begins to appear, the use of an English source, perhaps a version of the *Anglo-Saxon chronicle*, also seems likely; it is interesting, for example, that the chronicler describes William the Conqueror as having "subjected the English to perpetual slavery," and this perspective may have been adopted from an English source.[25] Certainly the use of one chronicle by another and the copying of material was a common occurrence in the production of such chronicles within the medieval tradition.[26]

There is no doubt, however, that the chroniclers also had access to other written information that does not now survive. This included royal and ecclesiastical letters and official documents, and the legalistic phraseology of the chronicle in several places betrays the use of this type of material. The entry for 1239, for example, relates how King Harald journeyed to Norway where he eventually received recognition and a grant of the Kingdom from King Hakon IV Hakonarson of Norway (r. 1217–1263):

> In the year 1239 Harald…went to the court of the Lord King of Norway, and there he stayed for two years and more. After such a long period with the king of Norway he finally found favour in his sight and he made him king over all the Isles which Godred, Reginald and Olaf, his predecessors, had possessed, and he confirmed them under the protection of his seal to him, his heirs and successors for ever.[27]

Similarly, under the year 1254 the chronicle relates how King Hakon, "established Magnus, son of Olaf, king over all the Isles which his predecessors possessed by right of inheritance and he confirmed them to him, and to his heirs and successors…by the protection of his seal forever."[28] The similarity of language in these entries to the formulaic and legalistic phraseology of contemporary documents as well as to each other makes it very likely indeed that the chronicler had access to the royal letters (or copies of them) in question,[29] and it is worth noting that monasteries in general and Cistercian houses in particular often possessed substantial archives. It has been observed that chronicles maintained by Cistercian monks are testament to this "bureaucratic mentality," and it may well have been the case that whenever a chronicle was composed it served as one component of a larger reference collection.[30] The copying of complete texts of letters and other similar documents into chronicles was common-place (sometimes preserving the texts of such documents for us when originals have long since vanished), although the Manx chronicle does not demonstrate this tendency to the same degree as other contemporary chronicles which often preserve full texts of entire documents. The Manx chronicle also makes reference to several other letters without, however, preserving their texts: a Norwegian royal letter is mentioned in 1250; a letter of King Rognvald's wife in 1223; and a letter sent to King Harald in 1248 which opposed the candidacy of Laurence, Archdeacon of Man, for the bishopric of the Isles.[31] It is tempting to suppose that at least some of these missives were known to the compilers, but this is speculation. It is worth noting here that scribes from medieval monasteries could be employed by rulers as clerks to produce the written instruments of gov-ernment that were becoming increasingly common in royal administration from the eleventh to thirteenth centuries.[32] In fact, a number of clerics are named in official documents of the Manx kings and could have played a role in the production and dissemination of written instruments at the Manx court in the twelfth and thirteenth centuries, and it is not beyond the realm of possibility that some of these scribes came from the monas-tery at Rushen.[33]

It has also been suggested that a now-lost Norse saga concerning the kings of Man and the Isles might have informed parts of the text.[34] Such a text does not now survive, but one section of the *Chronicles* which has the appearance of relying on a narrative like a saga is that detailing the massive struggle between the brothers Rognvald and Olaf throughout the 1220s. The relevant section begins with the unique remark from the compiler that, "for the benefit of readers it is considered not out of place now to relate briefly something about the deeds of the brothers Reginald and Olaf,"[35] which seems to be intended to draw attention to the significance of the discussion. Moreover, this is also the most detailed portion of the text, and it follows a tightly crafted story containing significant dramatic elements that possess some of the appearance of a saga. Whatever the case may be, it is certainly not beyond the realm of possibility that a saga of some or all of the Manx kings once existed, and the early thirteenth-century saga-history of the rulers of Orkney and Shetland, *Orkneyinga saga*, also known as *Jarls' saga*, provides a good analogue for a saga text relating the deeds of a dynasty of sea-lords who were contemporaries of the Manx kings. Like the *Chronicles*, it was written specifically to record the deeds of the jarls or earls.[36] It is also worth noting that *Orkneyinga saga* itself is thought to have utilized as a source a now-lost saga of Earl Harald Maddadson of Orkney and Caithness (d.c. 1206), *Haralds saga Maddaðarsonar*, which is preserved in part in its final chapters.[37] This demonstrates that such materials did, at one time, exist, even though they may no longer survive in their entirety, and it would not be surprising if materials of this sort underlay parts of the *Chronicles*.

Other types of material were also undoubtedly available and utilized by the compilers of the *Chronicles* as well, including ecclesiastical materials. The claim in the list of bishops appended to the *Chronicles* that the island was first converted by St. Patrick finds its parallel only in a *Life* of Saint Patrick compiled by the scholar Jocelin of Furness in c. 1185, and this has been taken to indicate that a local, Manx source may have been used by Jocelin as well. Similarly, the account of a miracle of St. Machutus which is inserted into the chronicle under the year 1158 and which relates how the saint drove off an army intent upon plundering the monastery (discussed further below) may well have drawn upon hagiographical material about St. Machutus available on the Island.[38]

In sum: the medieval text known as the *Chronicles of the Kings of Man and the Isles* is a thirteenth-century collaborative work compiled by several anonymous authors, and based upon a variety of sources, that serves as our main source for the history of the medieval Kingdom of Man and the Isles between the eleventh and early fourteenth centuries. It is not, however, an easy text to use and must be sifted carefully to determine the value of the evidence that it provides. Scholars remain divided on the historical value of the text. Some have concluded that, since the chronicle was composed so much later than many of the events that it describes, it cannot be considered a very reliable source, particularly for the early period.[39] Others, however, have concluded that the text was compiled with an historical purpose in mind and observed that the compilers seem to have been diligent and careful in their work.[40] Although there are some serious difficulties with the early period covered by the *Chronicles*, its value as an historical source increases as the account moves closer to the time of production; certainly the fact that the compilers had access to and made use of a range of different sources that have now vanished cannot be lightly dismissed. However challenging the chronicle is to utilize as an historical source, without it, our understanding of the period would be very much less clear.

We shall return to some key aspects of the chronicle and its composition later, but in the meantime, let us turn our attention back to the text, and to its account of the Manx kings with whom we begin our story.

Notes

1. G. Broderick, "Introduction," in G. Broderick (ed.), *Cronica Regum Mannie & Insularum. Chronicles of the Kings of Man and the Isles BL Cotton Julius A vii*, 2nd ed. (Douglas, 1995; repr. 1996), vii [hereafter *CRMI*]. The manuscript contains a number of separate items that were apparently bound together for the English scholar and bibliophile Sir Robert Cotton (d. 1631): see http://www.bl.uk/manuscripts/FullDisplay. aspx?ref=Cotton_MS_Julius_A_VII

2. See D.M. Wilson, *Manx Crosses. A Handbook of Stone Sculpture 500–1040 in the Isle of Man* (Oxford, 2018); K. Holman, *Scandinavian Runic Inscriptions in the British Isles: Their Historical Context* (Trondheim, 1996), 86–172. The classic work on the subject is P.M.C. Kermode, *Manx Crosses*, with an introduction by David M. Wilson (Balgavies, 1994).

3. C.W. Airne, *The Story of the Isle of Man, Volume 1. The Earliest Times to 1406* (Douglas, 1949), 27, where it is also observed that, "Unhappily, this record is in the possession, not of the Manx Museum, but of the British Museum" [now the British Library].

4. http://www.elginism.com/similar-cases/call-return-chronicles-man-british-library/20141205/7617/

5. Folios are different from pages: A folio is an individual leaf of paper or parchment, usually numbered only on the front (recto) face. Each folio has a front and a back, recto, and verso. In the case of the Manx chronicle the numbering of folios is not contemporary.

6. Broderick, "Introduction," *CRMI*, ix–x; B. Williams, "The Chronicles of the Kings of Man and the Isles," in S. Duffy and H. Mytum (eds.), *New History of the Isle of Man, Volume III: The Medieval Period 1000–1406* (Liverpool, 2015), 305–328. For more on palaeography and codicology see, for example, M.B. Parkes, *Their Hands Before Our Eyes: A Closer Look at Scribes. The Lyell Lectures Delivered in the University of Oxford 1999* (Aldershot and Burlington, VT, 2008).

7. *CRMI*, f. 49v.

8. A. Gransden, *Historical Writing in England c. 550–c. 1307* (Ithaca, 1974), 439 n.3.

9. *CRMI*, f. 49r, f. 49v ("home"); f. 34v (beauty).

10. *CRMI*, f. 32v, f. 33r, f. 40r; see also Williams, "Chronicles of the Kings of Man and the Isles," 310.

11. J. Harrison, "Cistercian Chronicling in the British Isles," in D. Broun and J. Harrison (eds.), *The Chronicle of Melrose Abbey a Stratigraphic Edition Volume 1: Introduction and Facsimile Edition* (Woodbridge, 2007), 14–18.

12. Harrison, "Cistercian Chronicling," 28.

13. See the excellent discussion on the motives for the production of chronicles in A. Gransden, "The Chronicles of Medieval England and Scotland," In A. Gransden (ed.), *Legends, Traditions and History in Medieval England* (London and Rio Grande, 1992), 208–218.

14. Williams, "Chronicles of the Kings of Man and the Isles," 310.

15. Harrison, "Cistercian Chronicling," 24.

16. *CRMI*, f. 35v–36r.

17. Compare B.T. Hudson, *Viking Pirates and Christian Princes: Dynasty, Religion, and Empire in the North Atlantic* (Oxford, 2005), 200 and Sir F.M. Powicke and E.B. Fryde, *Handbook of British Chronology*, 2nd ed. (London, 1961), 61.

18. *CRMI*, f. 50v.

19. Broderick, "Introduction," *CRMI*, xii–xiiv.

20. *CRMI*, f. 48r.

21. *CRMI*, f. 36v–f. 37r; see H. Birkett, *The Saints' Lives of Jocelin of Furness: Hagiography, Patronage and Ecclesiastical Politics* (Woodbridge, 2010), chapter 4 quote at 119.

22. Harrison, "Cistercian Chronicling," 27.

23. Harrison, "Cistercian Chronicling," 21–28.

24. "Introduction," in G. Broderick and B. Stowell (ed. and trans.), *Chronicle of the Kings of Mann and the Isles: Recortys Reeaghyn Vannin as ny h Ellanyn* (Edinburgh, 1973), vii–ix; see also A.G. Little, "The Authorship of the Lanercost Chronicle," *English Historical Review* 31 (1916), 269–279; and Williams, "Chronicles of the Kings of Man and the Isles," 315–317.

25. *CRMI*, f. 32v; Williams, "Chronicles of the Kings of Man and the Isles," 309–310.

26. Harrison, "Cistercian Chronicling," 25; see also A.A.M. Duncan, "Sources and Uses of the Chronicle of Melrose, 1165–1297," in S. Taylor (ed.), *Kings, Clerics and Chronicles in Scotland 500–1297: Essays in Honour of Marjorie Ogilvie Anderson on the Occasion of her Ninetieth Birthday* (Dublin, 2000), 146–186.

27. *CRMI*, f. 46r.

28. *CRMI*, f. 49r.

29. It is worth noting that belief in the existence of these documents, based upon the references in the *Chronicles*, is well-established in Norwegian historical scholarship: see for example *Regesta Norvegica I 822–1263*, ed. E. Gunnes (Oslo 1989).

30. Harrison, "Cistercian Chronicling," 22.

31. *CRMI*, f. 48v (1250); f. 42v (1223); f. 46v (1248).
32. R. Bartlett, *The Making of Europe: Conquest, Colonization and Cultural Change, 950–1350* (Princeton, 1993), 283–287, quotation at 285; see also K.J. Stringer, "Reform Monasticism and Celtic Scotland: Galloway, c.1140–c.1240," in E.J. Cowan and R.A. McDonald (eds.), *Alba: Celtic Scotland in the Medieval Era* (East Linton, 2000), 158.
33. R.A. McDonald, *Manx Kingship in Its Irish Sea Setting 1187–1229: King Rognvaldr and the Crovan Dynasty* (Dublin, 2007), 201–204.
34. Hudson, *Viking Pirates*, 9; E.J. Cowan, "The Last Kings of Man, 1229–1265," in S. Duffy and H. Mytum (eds.), *New History of the Isle of Man, Volume III: The Medieval Period 1000–1406* (Liverpool, 2015), 98.
35. *CRMI*, f. 41v.
36. B.E. Crawford, *The Northern Earldoms: Orkney and Caithness from AD 870 to 1470* (Edinburgh, 2013), 39–50.
37. M. Chesnutt, "Haralds saga Maddaðarsonar," in U. Dronke et al. (eds.), *Speculum Norroenum. Norse Studies in Memory of Gabriel Turville-Petre* (Odense, 1981), 33–55; Crawford, *Northern Earldoms*, 43.
38. See Birkett, *The Saints' Lives of Jocelin of Furness*, 42–44; M.T. Flanagan, "Jocelin of Furness and the Cult of St Patrick in Twelfth-Century Ulster," in C. Downham (ed.), *Jocelin of Furness Proceedings of the 2011 Conference* (Donington, 2013), 45–66 at 63 n 87.
39. S. Duffy, "Man and the Irish Sea World in the Eleventh Century," in S. Duffy and H. Mytum (eds.), *New History of the Isle of Man, Volume III: The Medieval Period 1000–1406* (Liverpool, 2015), 9.
40. Broderick, *CRMI*, xiv.

BIBLIOGRAPHY

Airne, C.W. 1949. *The Story of the Isle of Man, Volume 1. The Earliest Times to 1406*. Douglas.

Bartlett, R. 1993. *The Making of Europe: Conquest, Colonization and Cultural Change, 950–1350*. Princeton.

Birkett, H. 2010. *The Saints' Lives of Jocelin of Furness: Hagiography, Patronage and Ecclesiastical Politics*. Woodbridge.

Broderick, G. 1995. Introduction. In *Cronica Regum Mannie & Insularum. Chronicles of the Kings of Man and the Isles BL Cotton Julius A vii*, ed. G. Broderick, 2nd ed., vii–xvi. Douglas, repr. 1996; 1st ed., 1979.

Broderick, G., and B. Stowell. 1973. Introduction. In *Chronicle of the Kings of Mann and the Isles: Recortys Reeaghyn Vannin as ny hEllanyn*, ed. and trans. G. Broderick and B. Stowell, i–xi. Edinburgh.

Chesnutt, M. 1981. Haralds saga Maddaðarsonar. In *Speculum Norroenum. Norse Studies in Memory of Gabriel Turville-Petre*, ed. U. Dronke et al., 33–55. Odense.

Cowan, E.J. 2015. The Last Kings of Man, 1229–1265. In *New History of the Isle of Man, Volume III: The Medieval Period 1000–1406*, ed. S. Duffy and H. Mytum, 97–117. Liverpool.

Crawford, B.E. 2013. *The Northern Earldoms: Orkney and Caithness from AD 870 to 1470*. Edinburgh.

Duffy, S. 2015. Man and the Irish Sea World in the Eleventh Century. In *New History of the Isle of Man, Volume III: The Medieval Period 1000–1406*, ed. S. Duffy and H. Mytum, 9–26. Liverpool.

Duncan, A.A.M. 2000. Sources and Uses of the Chronicle of Melrose, 1165–1297. In *Kings, Clerics and Chronicles in Scotland 500–1297: Essays in Honour of Marjorie Ogilvie Anderson on the Occasion of Her Ninetieth Birthday*, ed. S. Taylor, 146–186. Dublin.

Flanagan, M.T. 2013. Jocelin of Furness and the Cult of St Patrick in Twelfth-Century Ulster. In *Jocelin of Furness Proceedings of the 2011 Conference*, ed. C. Downham, 45–66. Donington.

Gransden, A. 1974. *Historical Writing in England c. 550–c. 1307*. Ithaca.

———. 1992. The Chronicles of Medieval England and Scotland. In *Legends, Traditions and History in Medieval England*, ed. A. Gransden, 199–238. London and Rio Grande.

Harrison, J. 2007. Cistercian Chronicling in the British Isles. In *The Chronicle of Melrose Abbey a Stratigraphic Edition Volume 1: Introduction and Facsimile Edition*, ed. D. Broun and J. Harrison, 13–28. Woodbridge.

Holman, K. 1996. *Scandinavian Runic Inscriptions in the British Isles: Their Historical Context*. Trondheim.

Hudson, B.T. 2005. *Viking Pirates and Christian Princes: Dynasty, Religion, and Empire in the North Atlantic*. Oxford.

Kermode, P.M.C. 1994. *Manx Crosses*, with an introduction by David M. Wilson. Balgavies.

Little, A.G. 1916. The Authorship of the Lanercost Chronicle. *English Historical Review* 31: 269–279.

McDonald, R.A. 2007. *Manx Kingship in Its Irish Sea Setting 1187–1229: King Rognvaldr and the Crovan Dynasty*. Dublin.

Parkes, M.B. 2008. *Their Hands Before Our Eyes: A Closer Look at Scribes*, The Lyell Lectures Delivered in the University of Oxford 1999. Aldershot and Burlington, VT.

Powicke, F.M., and E.B. Fryde. 1961. *Handbook of British Chronology*. 2nd ed. London.

Regesta Norvegica I, 822–1263. 1989. Edited by E. Gunnes. Oslo.

Stringer, K.J. 2000. Reform Monasticism and Celtic Scotland: Galloway, c.1140–c.1240. In *Alba: Celtic Scotland in the Medieval Era*, ed. E.J. Cowan and R.A. McDonald, 127–165. East Linton.

Williams, B. 2015. The Chronicles of the Kings of Man and the Isles. In *New History of the Isle of Man, Volume III: The Medieval Period 1000–1406*, ed. S. Duffy and H. Mytum, 305–308. Liverpool.

Wilson, D.M. 2018. *Manx Crosses. A Handbook of Stone Sculpture 500–1040 in the Isle of Man.* Oxford.

WEBSITES

http://www.bl.uk/manuscripts/FullDisplay.aspx?ref=Cotton_MS_Julius_A_VII

http://www.elginism.com/similar-cases/call-return-chronicles-man-british-library/20141205/7617/

CHAPTER 3

Heroes: The Manx Sea Kings Descended from Godred Crovan

Abstract The principal focus of the *Chronicles of the Kings of Man and the Isles* is the dynasty of Manx sea kings that ruled Man and the Isles between 1079 and 1265 and from one perspective, the text can be regarded as a dynastic history. The early portion of the text dealing with the founder of the dynasty, the warlord Godred Crovan (d. 1095), proves challenging to sift for historical evidence and has the appearance of laying an ideological foundation for the dynasty's rule. By the early twelfth century material becomes more historical in nature and it is possible to examine the depiction of the Manx rulers by the compilers of the *Chronicles*.

Keywords *Chronicles of the Kings of Man and the Isles* • Godred Crovan • Crovan dynasty • Sea kings • Dynastic chronicle • Isle of Man

It has long been recognized that the principal focus of the *Chronicles* is the dynasty of Manx sea kings that ruled Man and the Isles between 1079 and 1265, and, as I will argue further below, the chronicle is closely entwined with the dynasty in several ways. In the meantime, however, our search for heroes and villains can begin with this dynasty and its rulers.

It has been observed that a chronicle tracing the history of a nation or royal family will often rely on legendary material[1] and it can be said that the earliest specifically Manx material in the *Chronicles* that relates to Godred Crovan conforms particularly well to this categorization. The

© The Author(s) 2019   21
R. A. McDonald, *Kings, Usurpers, and Concubines in the* Chronicles
of the Kings of Man and the Isles,
https://doi.org/10.1007/978-3-030-22026-6_3

Manx chronicle presents Godred as the semi-legendary founder of the dynasty who conquered the Isle of Man, settled in it, established new laws, and was the ancestor of subsequent kings. He is also presented as a great warlord who is said, somewhat enigmatically, to have "so tamed the Scots [perhaps Irish] that no one who built a ship or boat dared use more than three iron bolts."[2] When it comes to answering fundamental questions about who Godred was and the historicity of some of his actions, however, there is little else but the *Chronicles* to rely upon. The fact of Godred's existence is attested by his mention in Irish sources, which tell us that he conquered Dublin in 1091, was expelled in 1094, and died in 1095, but that is pretty well the sum of what we know about him. He is now regarded as being a member of the Hiberno-Norse dynasty of Dublin, probably the son of Ivar Haraldsson, king of Dublin from 1038 to 1046 (d. 1054), who was in turn the grandson of the famous Olaf Cuaran Sitricsson (d. 981).[3] Godred was therefore almost certainly a member of the powerful and influential Olafsson dynasty of Dublin, which had only recently fallen upon hard times in the super-competitive world of mid-eleventh century Irish politics. Among the most famous and prominent members of that dynasty was Sitric "Silkenbeard" Olafsson (d. 1042), ruler of Dublin from circa 989 to 1036, and so it can fairly be said that Godred was possessed of impeccable credentials.[4] Whoever he was, the account of Godred in the Chronicles highlights not only his importance as one of the great "heroes" of Manx history but also some of the challenges of untangling myth from history, and fact from legend, in the early part of this text.

The *Chronicles of the Kings of Man and the Isles* has sometimes been compared to the nearly contemporary saga-history of the rulers of Orkney and Shetland, *Orkneyinga saga*. It may well be that the early part of the *Chronicles*, and particularly its account of Godred Crovan and his conquest of the Isle of Man, is analogous to the early part of the saga which provides the mythical origins of the dynasty and represents "an important preliminary element in the historical account of the origins of the earldom dynasty," providing as it does "an irrefutable ideological foundation for the dynasty's power."[5] It is also worth noting that, like the Manx chronicle, which was compiled towards the end of the dynasty whose deeds it recorded, the redaction of the *Orkneyinga saga* that contains the mythical origins was written c. 1230, soon after the extinction of the Norse dynasty.[6] There is, then, good reason to think that the texts ought to be regarded in some sense as dynastic histories, and both belong more broadly to a range of thirteenth-century texts that were concerned with kingship in one way or another.

For some historians, Godred's greatest significance lies in the fact that he was the founder of a dynasty of sea kings who ruled in Man and the Hebrides for nearly two centuries following his death. It is also the case that when the *Chronicles* moves into the twelfth century and the reign of Olaf, the son of Godred, it seems to become more chronologically reliable and to move from the realm of legend into more solid historical footing. Thus the consolidation of the dynasty with Olaf seems to go hand in hand with the chronicle moving into more historical footing; from the reign of Olaf its chronology becomes more accurate, for example.

It is not possible, in the space available here, to provide a complete account of the kings descended from Godred Crovan that form the focus of the *Chronicles*. What follows is a brief historical overview of the kings with an emphasis upon their depiction in the *Chronicles*.[7]

The 20 years following Godred's death in 1095 were a turbulent and obscure period during which Manx, Hebridean, Irish, and Norwegian elements struggled for ascendency in Man and the Isles. Following the death of Godred, his sons Harald and Lagman fell to fighting amongst themselves over the prize of the kingship. Lagman, Godred's eldest son, is said to have seized the kingship in 1095, but his brother Harald rebelled against him, only to be captured and mutilated. Lagman, full of remorse for his actions, is subsequently said to have undertaken a pilgrimage to Jerusalem and to have died on the way. There are serious problems with interpreting the chronology presented by the chronicle at this point, however, and it may be that Lagman's supposed pilgrimage to Jerusalem actually represents participation in the Crusade of King Sigurd Jerusalem-Farer of Norway (d. 1130).[8] Whatever the case may be, both Irish and Norwegian elements also became involved in the struggles over Man and the Isles: the famous expedition of King Magnus III Barelegs of Norway (d. 1103) to the Isles in 1098 undoubtedly displaced native elements in Man and the Isles and may have left a physical mark in the region if Magnus constructed castles in the Isle of Man, as he is said to have done by the Chronicles: "He constructed fortresses there which to this day bear his name."[9]

After nearly 20 years of turbulence the dynasty of Godred Crovan was re-established on a firm footing by his son Olaf (c. 1113–1153). Olaf had been raised at the court of King Henry I of England (r. 1100–1135) and enjoyed a peaceful and prosperous reign. The Manx chronicle says of him that he "had all the kings of Ireland and Scotland as confederates in such a way that no one dared disturb the kingdom of the Isles during his lifetime."[10] Olaf's stature was reinforced by his generous patronage of the Church, and he was described as "devout and enthusiastic in matters of religion." One negative note is sounded when the *Chronicles* remark upon the fact that he "over-indulged in the domestic vice of kings,"[11] a reference to his keeping of concubines, a very important consideration to which we will return below. Olaf's reign came to an abrupt end in 1153 when he was slain by his brother's sons who had launched an invasion from Dublin.

Olaf was succeeded in the kingship by his son Godred (r. 1154–1187), whose reputation is more mixed than his father's. He was a powerful warlord who dealt ruthlessly with his father's killers and seemingly led an invasion of Ireland early in his reign, but the chronicle also critiques his tyrannical behaviour, which was to have catastrophic results for the Kingdom.[12] Still, the miracle of St. Machutus, who saved the monastery bearing his name from being plundered and helped to repel an invasion from the Hebrides led by Somerled, suggests that Godred was regarded as having had God on his side after all (further discussion below).

Godred seems to have introduced important innovations into succession and king—making practices in Man and the Isles. The *Chronicles* tell us that Godred sought, while still alive, to assure the succession of his younger son Olaf, because he had been born in lawful wedlock and the inheritance was his by right. But when Godred died in 1187 the Manx people opted instead for Olaf's brother, Rognvald, who, though older, does not seem to have been considered legitimate (more on this important point below). From this point onwards, a considerable proportion of the *Chronicles* is taken up with the events of King Rognvald's reign and especially the decades-long feud with his brother Olaf that resulted from the events surrounding the death of their father, Godred. Neither king comes off particularly badly in this section of the text: while Rognvald could conceivably be depicted as a usurper, it is instead emphasized that his selection as king was made by the Manx people, and his age and vigour are cited as the reasons why he was preferred. His death in battle at Tynwald in February 1229 was said to have been perpetrated by a band of wicked men, and treachery is implied; the *Chronicles* seem a little sympathetic here and also somewhat critical of Olaf, remarking that, "he never in his lifetime exacted vengeance" for Rognvald's death.[13] Olaf's sole reign from 1229 until 1237 is, perhaps curiously, covered very briefly in only a few lines of text. But the *Chronicles* nevertheless seem to suggest that he was the rightful king since he is said to have "recovered his inheritance" in 1226 when the Manx people, angered by a tax levied by Rognvald, drove him out and accepted Olaf as king instead.[14] This provides an important insight into partisanship in the Chronicle, to which we shall return in due course.

Following the death of Olaf, his three sons ruled in turn: Harald (r. 1237–1248), Reginald (Rognvald) (r. May 1249), and Magnus (r. 1252–1265).[15] A significant theme across all three reigns is the relationship with Norway and its mighty king, Hakon IV Hakonarson (r. 1217–1263), whose long reach into the Isles was demonstrated on several occasions. It was not until the early 1240s, about four years after his succession to the kingship, that Harald received ratification from King Hakon, but from then onwards his reign is presented as peaceful and stable and Harald is depicted as being internationally respected. The *Chronicles* remark: "And so from that time he began ruling quietly and peacefully in Man, and held a very stable peace with the king of England and the king of Scotland, and was an ally of theirs in friendship."[16] Following his premature death by drowning in a shipwreck off Sumburgh Head in Shetland (noted at the Introduction of this work), we are told that, "His death was a cause of grief to all who had known him."[17] This comment is neatly paralleled in the nearly contemporary *Saga of King Hakon*, composed by the Icelander Sturla Thordarson in the years following King Hakon's death in 1263, where we are told that the loss of the ship was "the greatest harm and ill-luck to the South-islanders that they lost so suddenly such a prince, when his voyage to Norway had been so lucky…"[18]

From the death of Harald in 1248 until the establishment of his brother Magnus in the kingship in 1252, the *Chronicles* relate the deadly game of Manx thrones referred to at the outset of this study. Harald was succeeded by his brother Reginald, who was slain mere weeks into his reign by the knight Ivar. Following his death, Harald, the son of Godred Don, an illegitimate son of King Rognvald, took the kingship. The *Chronicles* demonize him as an usurper, not least through the use of a miracle story which demonstrates his treachery and shows that God is on the side of the rightful line of kings descended from Olaf. Harald was eventually removed from power by King Hakon in 1250 or 1251, and, following further struggles, Magnus was at last firmly established in the kingship in 1254. The *Chronicles* at this point emphasize the status of Magnus as the rightful king; he was allowed to return to Man from Norway "with great honour," while a trip to England in 1256 resulted in "much honour and precious gifts" from Henry III of England (r. 1216–1272).[19]

Magnus' death without legitimate male heirs in November 1265 at Castle Rushen in the Isle of Man signalled the end of the dynasty's reign in Man and the Isles, but it is interesting that, while the *Chronicles* record his death, they pass over its significance in near silence.[20] The full significance of Magnus's death as an historical milestone was, however, captured by a set of annals compiled across the Irish Sea at Furness Abbey in Cumbria, which observed that, with the death of Magnus, "kings ceased to reign in Man."[21]

Remaining entries in the *Chronicles* up to the early fourteenth century record the "transfer" of the Kingdom of Man and the Isles to the Scottish king in 1266; a Scottish invasion in 1275 to suppress a Manx uprising against Scottish overlordship (discussed further below); a record of the invasion of Man by Robert Bruce in 1313, and the final entry records an invasion of Man in 1316 from Ireland. The entry ends on a depressing note, recording the plunder of the Island and Rushen Abbey at the hands of the invaders:

> They plundered the land of all its more valuable goods and came upon much silver which had been long hidden in many places throughout the country. After this they came to Rushen Abbey and plundered both its furnishings and its cattle and sheep, that they left nothing at all. And when they had spent a month at such activities they loaded their ships with the more valuable assets of the country and in this way returned home.[22]

NOTES

1. N.F. Blake, "Chronicles," in J.R. Strayer (ed.), *Dictionary of the Middle Ages*, 12 vols. (New York, 1983), vol. 3, 327.

2. *Cronica Regum Mannie & Insularum. Chronicles of the Kings of Man and the Isles BL Cotton Julius A vii*, ed. G. Broderick, 2nd ed. (Douglas, 1995; repr. 1996; 1st ed. 1979), f. 33r–33v. [Hereafter *CRMI*].

3. B.T. Hudson, *Viking Pirates and Christian Princes: Dynasty, Religion, and Empire in the North Atlantic* (Oxford, 2005), 171. See also S. Duffy "Man and the Irish Sea World in the Eleventh Century," in S. Duffy and H. Mytum (eds.), *A New History of the Isle of Man, Volume III. The Medieval Period 1000–1406* (Liverpool, 2015), 9–26.

4. S. Duffy, "Emerging from the Mist: Ireland and Man in the Eleventh Century," in P.J. Davey and D. Finlayson (eds.), *Mannin Revisited: Twelve Essays on Manx Culture and Environment* (Edinburgh, 2002), 55–56. Duffy regards Godred as a son or nephew of Ivar Haraldsson. See also G. Broderick, "Irish and Welsh Strands in the Geneaology of Godred Crovan," *Journal of the Manx Museum* 8 (1980), 32–38.

5. B.E. Crawford, *The Northern Earldoms: Orkney and Caithness from AD 870 to 1470* (Edinburgh, 2013), 80.

6. Crawford, *Northern Earldoms*, 80 and n. 2; background on *Orkneyinga saga* in M. Chesnutt, *"Orkneyinga Saga"* in P. Pulsiano (ed.), *Medieval Scandinavia: An Encyclopedia* (New York, 1993), 456–457, and the relevant comments in J. Jesch, "History in the 'Political Sagas,'" *Medium Aevum* 62 (1993), 210–220.

7. On these kings in general see R.A. McDonald, *The Sea Kings: The Late Norse Kingdoms of Man and the Isles, c. 1066–1275* (Edinburgh, 2019). Other studies include S. Duffy and H. Mytum (eds.), *New History of the Isle of Man, Volume III: The Medieval Period 1000–1406* (Liverpool, 2015), which covers the entire period of the Kingdom of Man and the Isles; R.A. McDonald, *Manx Kingship in its Irish Sea Setting 1187–1229: King Rognvaldr and the Crovan Dynasty* (Dublin, 2007); I. Beuermann, *Man amongst the Kings and Bishops: What was the Reason for Godred Olafsson's Journey to Norway in 1152/53?* (Oslo, 2002); and see also Hudson, *Viking Pirates*.

8. *CRMI*, f. 33v; Hudson, *Viking Pirates*, 188–189, 198–199.

9. *CRMI* f. 34v. On Magnus see R. Power, "The Isle of Man and the Kings of Norway: Magnús Barelegs and After," in Duffy and Mytum (eds.), *New History of the Isle of Man III*, 27–57; R. Power, "Magnus Barelegs' Expeditions to the West," *Scottish Historical Review* 73 (1985), 107–132; and Hudson, *Viking Pirates*, 189–198. On the identification of castles in Man that might be associated with his expedition, see P. Davey, *After the Vikings: Medieval Archaeology of the Isle of Man AD 1100–1550* (Douglas, 2013), 41–47.

10. *CRMI*, f. 35v.

11. *CRMI*, f. 35v.

12. *CRMI*, f. 37v.

13. *CRMI*, f. 44v.

14. *CRMI*, f. 43v. Rognvald's reign is covered in detail in McDonald, *Manx Kingship*, but see also R. Costain-Russell, "The Reigns of Guðröðr and Rögnvaldr, 1153–1229," in S. Duffy and H. Mytum (eds.), *New History of the Isle of Man, Volume III: The Medieval Period 1000–1406* (Liverpool, 2015), 79–96.

15. See inter alia E.J. Cowan, "The Last Kings of Man, 1229–1265," in Duffy and Mytum (eds.), *New History of the Isle of Man Volume III*, 97–117.

16. *CRMI*, f. 46r

17. *CRMI*, f. 47r

18. *The Saga of Hakon, and a Fragment of the Saga of Magnus, with Appendices,* trans. Sir G.W. Dasent. *Icelandic Sagas and Other Historical Documents Relating to the Settlements and Descents of the Northmen on the British Isles* (London, 1894), vol. 4, 267–268, chapter 261. The modern edition of the text is *Hákonar saga Hákonarsonar*, eds. Þ. Hauksson, S. Jakobsson, and T. Ulset, 2 vols. (Reykjavík, 2013); there is no modern translation.

19. *CRMI*, f. 49r–f. 49v. English government documents corroborate the claim: a letter of protection for Magnus from April 1256 describes the Manx king as "lately invested with a military belt": *Foedera, conventiones, litterae, et cujuscunque generis acta publica, inter reges Angliae et alios quosvis imperatores, reges, pontifices, principes, vel communitates habita aut tractata*, ed. T. Rymer, 10 vols. (Hagae Comitis, 1739–1745), i, pt. ii, 12; *Monumenta de Insula Manniae, or a Collection of National Documents Relating to the Isle of Man*, ed. and trans. J.R. Oliver, 3 vols. (Douglas, 1860–1862), ii, 86.

20. Similarly, the famous expedition of King Hakon IV of Norway in 1263 also receives only the briefest of mentions: "In the year of our Lord 1263 Hakon King of Norway came to Scotland and achieving nothing returned to Orkney and there died at Kirkwall," *CRMI*, f. 49v.

21. *Annals of Furness* in *Chronicles of the Reigns of Stephen, Henry II and Richard I*, ed. R. Howlett, 4 vols. (London, 1884–1849), ii, 549; trans. *Scottish Annals from English Chroniclers, A.D. 500–1286*, ed. and trans. A.O. Anderson (London, 1908; repr. Stamford 1991), 380.

22. *CRMI*, f. 50r; see C. McNamee, "The Isle of Man under Scottish Rule, 1266–1333," in Duffy and Mytum (eds.), *New History of the Isle of Man, Volume III*, 118–150.

BIBLIOGRAPHY

Beuermann, I. 2002. *Man amongst the Kings and Bishops: What was the Reason for Godred Olafsson's Journey to Norway in 1152/53?* Oslo.

Blake, N.F. 1983. Chronicles. In *Dictionary of the Middle Ages*, ed. J.R. Strayer, vol. 3, 12 vols., 325–330. New York.

Broderick, G. 1980. Irish and Welsh Strands in the Geneaology of Godred Crovan. *Journal of the Manx Museum* 8: 32–38.

Chesnutt, M. 1993. Orkneyinga Saga. In *Medieval Scandinavia: An Encyclopedia*, ed. P. Pulsiano, 456–457. New York.

Chronicles of the Reigns of Stephen, Henry II and Richard I. 1884–1889. Edited by R. Howlett, 4 vols. London.

Costain-Russell, R. 2015. The Reigns of Guðröðr and Rögnvaldr, 1153–1229. In *New History of the Isle of Man, Volume III: The Medieval Period 1000–1406*, ed. S. Duffy and H. Mytum, 79–96. Liverpool.

Cowan, E.J. 2015. The Last Kings of Man, 1229–1265. In *New History of the Isle of Man, Volume III: The Medieval Period 1000–1406*, ed. S. Duffy and H. Mytum, 97–117. Liverpool.

Crawford, B.E. 2013. *The Northern Earldoms: Orkney and Caithness from AD 870 to 1470.* Edinburgh.

Cronica Regum Mannie & Insularum. Chronicles of the Kings of Man and the Isles BL Cotton Julius A vii. 1995. Edited by G. Broderick, 2nd ed. Douglas; repr. 1996.

Davey, P. 2013. *After the Vikings: Medieval Archaeology of the Isle of Man AD 1100–1550.* Douglas.

Duffy, S. 2002. Emerging from the Mist: Ireland and Man in the Eleventh Century. In *Mannin Revisited: Twelve Essays on Manx Culture and Environment*, ed. P.J. Davey and D. Finlayson, 53–61. Edinburgh.

———. 2015. Man and the Irish Sea World in the Eleventh Century. In *New History of the Isle of Man, Volume III: The Medieval Period 1000–1406*, ed. S. Duffy and H. Mytum, 9–26. Liverpool.

Foedera, conventiones, litterae, et cujuscunque generis acta publica, inter reges Angliae et alios quosvis imperatores, reges, pontifices, principes, vel communitates habita aut tractata. 1739–1745. Edited by T. Rymer, 10 vols. Hagae Comitis.

Hákonar saga Hákonarsonar. 2013. Edited by. Þ. Hauksson, S. Jakobsson, and T. Ulset, 2 vols. Reykjavík.

Hudson, B.T. 2005. *Viking Pirates and Christian Princes: Dynasty, Religion, and Empire in the North Atlantic.* Oxford.

Jesch, J. 1993. History in the 'Political Sagas'. *Medium Aevum* 62: 210–220.

McDonald, R.A. 2007. *Manx Kingship in its Irish Sea Setting 1187–1229: King Rognvaldr and the Crovan Dynasty.* Dublin.

———. 2019. *The Sea Kings: The Late Norse Kingdoms of Man and the Isles, c. 1066–1275.* Edinburgh.

McNamee, C. 2015. The Isle of Man under Scottish Rule, 1266–1333. In *New History of the Isle of Man, Volume III: The Medieval Period 1000–1406*, ed. S. Duffy and H. Mytum, 118–150. Liverpool.

Monumenta de Insula Manniae, or a Collection of National Documents Relating to the Isle of Man. 1860–1862. Edited and translated by J.R. Oliver, 3 vols. Douglas.

A New History of the Isle of Man, Volume III. The Medieval Period 1000–1406. 2015. Edited by S. Duffy and H. Mytum. Liverpool.

Power, R. 1985. Magnus Barelegs' Expeditions to the West. *Scottish Historical Review* 73: 107–132.

————. 2015. The Isle of Man and the Kings of Norway: Magnús Barelegs and After. In *New History of the Isle of Man, Volume III: The Medieval Period 1000–1406*, ed. S. Duffy and H. Mytum, 27–57. Liverpool.

The Saga of Hakon, and a Fragment of the Saga of Magnus, with Appendices. 1894. Translated by Sir G.W. Dasent. *Icelandic Sagas and Other Historical Documents Relating to the Settlements and Descents of the Northmen on the British Isles*, vol. 4. London.

Scottish Annals from English Chroniclers, A.D. 500–1286. 1908. Edited and translated by A.O. Anderson. London; repr. Stamford 1991.

CHAPTER 4

Villains: Rivals for the Kingdom

Abstract If the Manx sea kings descended from Godred Crovan represent the heroes of the *Chronicles*, the territorial rivals of these kings are depicted unfavourably in the text. These include Somerled (d. 1164), the ruler of Argyll and Kintyre, and his descendants, whose rise is claimed to have caused the break-up of the Kingdom, as well as the Scottish kings Alexander II and III, whose territorial ambitions in the western seaboard caused the Kingdom of Man and the Isles to be integrated into the Scottish Kingdom. The *Chronicles of the Kings of Man and the Isles* presents a unique Manx perspective on significant developments in twelfth- and thirteenth-century Scottish history.

Keywords *Chronicles of the Kings of Man and the Isles* • Somerled of Argyll • MacSorleys • Kings of Scots • Alexander II • Alexander III

If the Manx kings descended from Godred Crovan represent the heroes of the Chronicle (at least as we understand it for now) then we might expect that the villains of the text are those who would challenge the Manx kings or otherwise rival them for control of the Kingdom.

R. A. McDonald, *Kings, Usurpers, and Concubines in the* Chronicles of the Kings of Man and the Isles, https://doi.org/10.1007/978-3-030-22026-6_4

4.1   SOMERLED AND HIS DESCENDANTS

One such figure, and a famous and significant figure in Hebridean and Irish Sea history in his own right, is Somerled (d. 1164), described in the *Chronicles* as the "ruler of Argyll" and in Irish sources as *rí Innsi Gall & Cind tíre*, "King of the Hebrides and Kintyre."[1] Somerled makes an early appearance in the *Chronicles* when we are told that he married one of Olaf's daughters by a concubine, and then a little later, in the entries for 1156 and 1158, when Somerled's defeat of King Godred Olafsson, the ensuing division of the Kingdom, and Godred's flight to Norway are all related:

> In the year 1156 a naval battle was fought on the night of the Epiphany (6 January) between Godred and Somerled and there was much slaughter on both sides. When day dawned they made peace and divided the kingdom of the Isles between them. The kingdom has existed in two parts from that day up until the present time, and this was the cause of the break-up of the kingdom from the time the sons of Somerled got possession of it.[2]

The *Chronicles* thus present Somerled not only as the founder of a rival dynastic line in the Isles, but also as bearing some responsibility for fracturing the unity of the Kingdom, effectively dividing it into two rival Kingdoms of the Isles, a split that endured until the end of both Kingdoms in the 1260s.[3] It is therefore no surprise that Somerled, his descendants, and his followers, are presented in a consistently poor light throughout the *Chronicles*, and assume their place as some of the principal villains of the text.

This vilification may be seen to best effect in an anecdote in the *Chronicles* relating to the plundering of the monastery of St. Machutus to which we will return in Chap. 5 below, but the descendants of Somerled also appear in a negative light elsewhere in the text. For instance, in 1250, as part of the ongoing struggles over the kingship between the descendants of Rognvald and Olaf, Harald, the son of Godred Don, son of Rognvald, seized the kingship but was summoned to Norway to answer for his actions. That same year Magnus, son of Olaf, along with "John son of Dougal" arrived in Man, with Norwegian support. The individual styled "John son of Dougal" by the chronicler was Ewen the son of Duncan (d.c. 1268), a great-grandson of Somerled and a figure of considerable importance in the Hebrides as the head of the most prominent of

Somerled's descendants in the thirteenth century, the MacDougalls. Ewen was a major contender for power in the Isles from the late 1240s to the 1260s, and he appears to have been given some form of authority in the Southern Isles following the drowning of Harald of Man off Sumburgh Head in late 1248 en route from Norway to Man.[4] He is depicted as behaving arrogantly in the Chronicle under the year 1250, where we are told that:

> John, son of Dougal sent envoys to the people of Man who said, "John, king of the Isles, orders you to do this and this." When the Manxmen heard John being called king of the Isles and not Magnus son of Olaf they were very angry and refused to hear the envoys' words further...[5]

The ire of the Manx led to stout resistance, and Ewen and his allies were ignominiously driven off; many were killed, and others were drowned in a shipwreck as they departed. The chronicler states that, "I have no doubt that they got their deserts because of their pride and haughtiness, in that because they refused to accept the peace (terms) offered to them by the people of the land."[6] The episode highlights not merely antipathy to Ewen as an interloper in the kingship, but also simultaneously emphasizes the rightful claim of Magnus to the Manx kingship—a prominent theme in the second half of the *Chronicles* and one to which we shall return shortly.

The attitude of the *Chronicles* towards Somerled and his descendants offers an informative case-study in the importance of perspective in history, since, although Somerled is reviled by the chronicler as causing the break-up of the Kingdom of the Isles, his reputation in Scottish history is something quite different—that of a founder rather than a destroyer. As the progenitor of several powerful and significant West Highland families that dominated the region for centuries after his death, including the MacDonalds, MacDougalls, and MacRuairis, Somerled emerged by the late middle ages as a great hero of the Scottish Gàidhealtachd: a powerful Gaelic lord intent upon driving out the Norse and establishing an independent Gaelic Kingdom in the west. It is in this guise that he frequently appears in more recent popular and clan histories.[7] In fact, of course, Somerled's own name was Norse (*Sumarliði*, from Old Norse "Summer voyager," a kenning (poetic circumlocution) for "Viking"; it is one of many Gaelic names ultimately derived from Old Norse), and his origins and ancestry were firmly rooted in the mixed Gaelic-Norse milieu of the Hebrides—the same milieu from which the Manx sea kings sprang.[8] The evidence of early thirteenth-century praise-poetry compiled for some of Somerled's descendants suggests that, at that time, at least, "members of Clann Somairle saw their recent heritage as coming from the *Gaill* [foreigners, i.e. the Norse]."[9] It is of more than passing interest that this poetry highlights the position of Godred Crovan as the great-grandfather of Somerled's sons.[10] Thus, at more or less the same time at which the Manx chronicle was vilifying Somerled and his descendants as the cause of the downfall of the Kingdom, Somerled's own descendants were patronizing Gaelic bards who composed verses celebrating their descent from Godred Crovan! A panegyric on Angus son of Donald, for instance, celebrates his lineage as, "the House of Somhairle, the race of Gofraidh, from whom you came…" [11] This demonstrates the extent to which pedigrees and genealogies could be regularly reworked and manipulated, largely for political purposes, in the period under consideration.[12]

4.2   THE KINGS OF SCOTS

If Somerled and his descendants are depicted in a negative light throughout the *Chronicles*, the thirteenth-century Scottish kings Alexander II (r. 1214–1249) and Alexander III (r. 1249–1286) also receive less than favourable treatment. This is perhaps unsurprising, since these rulers are well known for their achievement of annexing the Hebrides and the Isle of Man for Scotland—a process famously described as "the winning of the West" by one prominent modern Scottish historian.[13] Key stages in the process occurred in the reign of Alexander II, who died at Kerrera in 1249 in the midst of a significant campaign against the chieftains of the western seaboard.[14] His son Alexander III succeeded as a minor but upon assuming personal control of government in 1260 made it clear that he intended to continue his father's policies where the western seaboard was concerned. Diplomatic overtures to King Hakon IV of Norway in the early 1260s were rebuffed, and King Hakon's massive expeditionary force of 1263, hampered by poor weather, was repelled by the Scots in 1263, although the so-called "battle" of Largs was not nearly the great Scottish victory that it is sometimes described as.[15] Nevertheless, the Treaty of Perth in 1266 ceded the Hebrides and the Isle of Man to Scotland from Norway. By then, the last Manx king, Magnus, had died (1265), having already, in 1264, submitted to Alexander III.[16] The Manx chronicle notes the death of Magnus and his burial at Rushen Abbey with no further comment, but a series of annals compiled at Furness Abbey, across the Irish Sea from Man and well-connected through ties of patronage to the Manx dynasty and to Rushen Abbey, added the important comment that "kings ceased to reign in Man."[17]

Although the acquisition of the Isles for Scotland (famously described by the prominent Scottish medievalist Professor Geoffrey Barrow as "the winning of the west"[18]) is often lauded as a great accomplishment of these two famous thirteenth-century Scottish monarchs, and the reign of Alexander III is sometimes characterized as representing a "Golden Age" in Scottish history,[19] it is not difficult to see why the matter might appear rather different from a Manx perspective, and it is therefore hardly surprising that the *Chronicles* harbour a certain amount of resentment towards what might be described as Scottish imperialism in the Isles. Although the *Chronicles* say relatively little about Alexander II's abortive campaign of 1249, which was brought to an abrupt halt by the king's death on Kerrera, they do provide an important comment on Alexander's motivation, remarking that "he wanted to subject to his sway the kingdom of all the Isles."[20]

This statement is particularly interesting because Alexander's covetousness is highlighted in another late thirteenth-century text that demonstrates considerable interest in the Hebrides and the Isle of Man—the *Saga of King Hakon*, composed by the Icelander Sturla Thordarson (d.1284) within a few years of the death of King Hakon in 1263. It has been suggested that Sturla identified with the dilemma of the Hebridean chieftains as they found themselves ground between Scottish and Norwegian royal authority in the middle of the thirteenth century, and the saga seems to come close to articulating a Hebridean perspective on events.[21] It is interesting, then, that the comment of the *Chronicles* to the effect that Alexander sought subjugation of the Isles is repeated almost verbatim in the saga, where it is stated that, "Alexander the Scot-king was very greedy for the realm in the southern Isles."[22] The saga continues: "He gave it out to his men that he did not mean to stay his course till he had planted his banner east of Thursa Skerries [in Shetland], and won under him all the realm of the king of Norway which he owned to the west of Solund Sea."[23] Elsewhere in the saga, when he first appears in the text, Alexander is described as "a great prince and very greedy of this world's honour."[24] It's probably worth noting that the composition of the saga is almost contemporary with that of the *Chronicles*, and so given the similarity of comment about Alexander's covetousness one can't help but wonder about the flow of information back and forth along the sea-road

between Norway, the Hebrides, and Man, and therefore also about the
extent to which one text may have been influenced by the other. Indeed,
since the *Chronicles'* entries for 1263, 1265, 1266, and 1274 were written
by a second scribe, they are exactly contemporary with *King Hakon's saga*.
Whatever the case may be, there seems little question that Sturla had
access to first-hand information, probably derived from participants in
King Hakon's ill-fated expedition of 1263 as they returned to Norway,[25]
and the similarity of perspective in the *Chronicles* and the saga is striking.

As we might expect, the *Chronicles* have little to say about the cession
of the Isle of Man to Scotland in 1266, observing merely that "the
Kingdom of Man and the Isles was transferred to Alexander King of the
Scots."[26] The next entry but one, however, strikes a different tone:[27]

> In the year of our Lord 1275 on the seventh day of the month of October
> the fleet of Lord Alexander King of Scotland landed at Ronaldsway in Man,
> and the following day before sunrise a battle was fought between the
> Manxmen and the Scots; but the Scots were victorious and they cut down
> five hundred and thirty seven of the Manxmen in that conflict, wherefore a
> certain rhymster (writes):
>
> > Ten times 50, three times 10, and five and two did fall,
> > O Manx race, beware lest future catastrophe you befall.

Further details, lacking in the *Chronicles*, are to be found in other contemporary sources, particularly the northern English *Chronicle of Lanercost*.
Its entry for the year 1275 provides the vital information that the invasion
was prompted by an uprising in the name of Godfrey, a son of Magnus,
who, "they [the Manx] had a little while before set up to be their king."
According to *Lanercost*, a Scottish embassy to Godfrey was rebuffed, the
battle ensued, and "the wretched Manxmen turned their backs, and perished miserably."[28]

Of particular interest here is the Manx chronicle's reference to the
verses: as noted above, it was by no means unusual for a chronicle to incor-
porate verses, either specially composed for the purpose, or already in existence. It is impossible to know whether the verses might have been
composed specifically for the *Chronicles* or were already in circulation;
either is possible, but a Manx provenance for them seems virtually certain,
given the tone of the second line—"O Manx race, beware lest future catas-
trophe you befall."[29] The prophetic nature of the verses calls to mind the

Scottish poet and prophet Thomas the Rhymer, also known as Thomas of Erceldoune (fl. late thirteenth century), who is said, in a fifteenth-century source, to have predicted the death of King Alexander III of Scotland in 1286 (although no sources contemporary with his lifetime attribute prophecies to him)[30]:

> Do you not remember what the country prophet Thomas de Earlston had said to the earl of March at Dunbar Castle when he obscurely prophesied concerning the king's end the night before the death of King Alexander? The earl had asked him, half-jesting as usual, what news the next day would bring. Thomas gave a sobbing sigh from the depths of his heart, and is said to have made this clear pronouncement to the earl in front of his retainers: 'Alas for tomorrow, a day of calamity and misery! because before the stroke of twelve a strong wind will be heard in Scotland the like of which has not been known since times long ago, Indeed its blast will dumb-found the nations and render senseless those who hear it; it will humble what is lofty and raze what is unbending to the ground.'[31]

The Manx chronicle's entry for 1275 must be understood against the backdrop of the Scottish annexation of the Isle of Man in the previous decade. As noted above, Alexander and the Scots forced King Magnus into submission in 1264, and Man was firmly subdued by an invasion in 1265 following Magnus's death. A Scottish document dated between 1266 and 1284 refers to Alexander (d. 1284), the eldest son of Alexander III, as "lord of Man" (*dominus Mannie*), and the Isle of Man seems to have been treated as the appanage of the heir to the Scottish throne, the elder son of the Scottish king.[32] Administration of the Island was entrusted to a series of bailies, and it seems clear that Scottish rule was resented.[33] The *Annals of Furness* provide further details about Godred son of Magnus, the focal point of the uprising of 1275, stating that he was an illegitimate son of Magnus who had come to Man in the aftermath of Magnus's death and the cession of Man and the Hebrides to Scotland.[34] These annals also state that Godred was not killed in the battle of 1275, but managed to flee with his wife to Wales; it is in fact quite likely that he had arrived from Wales as well, since the Manx dynasty was possessed of links to north Wales.[35] The Furness annals also exhibit sympathy for the Manx, particularly in their account of the slaughter of the unarmed Manx by the Scots in 1275:

...So a battle was fought, and the Manxmen, unarmed and naked, could not resist the slingers, ballistaries, archers and armed men, and fled with Godfrey their king. And the others pursuing them cut down and slew man and beast, as many as they could catch, sparing not for sex or place ... And the enemy aforesaid despoiled the abbey of Rushen and the monks, and sent them away almost naked. And at that time perished miserably all the nobles and the captains, and also the rest of the people, whose exact number no one knows. And thus was the land destroyed and despoiled.[36]

A letter addressed to the English king on behalf of the inhabitants of the Isle of Man in 1290 struck a similar note when it referred to the island as "lately desolate and full of wretchedness."[37] It seems, therefore, that Manx tradition was hostile to the two Alexanders and the Scots in the late thirteenth and early fourteenth centuries—and there is some evidence for this apart from the *Chronicles*. It is, for example, interesting and significant that the abbot of Rushen described Alexander III as having "conquered the Isle of Man by the sword" (*qui Insulam de Manne per ensem conquestabatur*) in the course of early fourteenth-century legal proceedings.[38] By then, of course, the Isle of Man had been a strategic prize hotly contested between England and Scotland and had changed hands, sometimes in rapid succession, on several occasions.[39]

The final entries in the Manx chronicle relate to the struggles over the Isle of Man between English and Scots that formed part of the Irish Sea theatre of war of the Wars of Scotland in the early fourteenth century. Here again we see the Scottish hero-king Robert Bruce (Robert I; r. 1306–1329) as the aggressor:

In the year of our Lord 1313 Lord Robert King of Scotland landed at Ramsey with a host of ships, that is on the 18th day of May, and on the Sunday following he went to the nunnery at Douglas where he spent the night. On the Monday following he laid siege to Castle Rushen which Lord Dougal Mac Dowyl held against the said Lord King until the Tuesday next after the following feast of St. Barnabas the Apostle (11 June); and the same day the Lord King took the said castle.[40]

Thus, the *Chronicles* conclude on a despairing note, recording the subjugation of the Island by the Scottish king Robert I as part of the Anglo-Scottish conflicts of the early fourteenth century.[41]

NOTES

1. W. Stokes, ed. and trans. "The Annals of Tigernach," *Revue Celtique* 18 (1897), 9–59, 150–303 at 195; electronic version online at CELT: Corpus of Electronic Texts: A Project of University College Cork College Road, Cork, Ireland (2010) at http://www.ucc.ie/celt/published/T100002A/index.html

2. *Cronica Regum Mannie & Insularum. Chronicles of the Kings of Man and the Isles BL Cotton Julius A vii*, ed. G. Broderick, 2nd ed. (Douglas, 1995; repr. 1996; 1st ed. 1979), f. 37v [hereafter *CRMI*].

3. On Somerled and his descendants see W.D.H. Sellar, "Hebridean Sea Kings: The Successors of Somerled, 1164–1316," in E.J. Cowan and R.A. McDonald (eds.), *Alba: Celtic Scotland in the Medieval Era* (East Linton, 2000), 187–218; R.A. McDonald, *The Sea Kings: The Late Norse Kingdoms of Man and the Isles, c. 1066–1275* (Edinburgh, 2019), chapter 5; and R.A. McDonald, *The Kingdom of the Isles: Scotland's Western Seaboard, c. 1100–c. 1336* (East Linton, 1997).

4. *The Saga of Hakon, and a Fragment of the Saga of Magnus, with Appendices*, trans. Sir G.W. Dasent. *Icelandic Sagas and Other Historical Documents Relating to the Settlements and Descents of the Northmen on the British Isles* (London, 1894), vol. 4, 270, chapter 264. The modern edition of the text is *Hákonar saga Hákonarsonar*, eds. Þ. Hauksson, S. Jakobsson, and T. Ulset, 2 vols. (Reykjavík, 2013); there is no modern translation.

5. *CRMI*, f. 48r–48v.

6. *CRMI*, f. 48v.

7. The traditional view is represented by the seventeenth-century "History of the MacDonalds," in *Highland Papers*, ed. J.R.N. MacPhail, 4 vols. (Edinburgh, 1914–1934), i, 5–9; cf. K. MacPhee, *Somerled: Hammer of the Norse* (Castle Douglas, 2004); but compare, for example, McDonald, *Kingdom of the Isles*, chapter 2, and see further n. 8 below.

8. See McDonald, *Kingdom of the Isles*, chapter 2; R.A. McDonald, "Man, Somerled, and the Isles: The Rise of a New Dynasty," in S. Duffy and H. Mytum (eds.), *New History of the Isle of Man Volume III: The Medieval Period 1000–1406* (Liverpool, 2015), 58–78. Recent genetic studies indicate that Somerled was of Norse ancestry: B. Sykes, *The Blood of the Isles: Exploring the Genetic Roots of Our Tribal History* (London, 2006), 254–262, and B. Sykes, *Adam's Curse: A Future Without Men* (New York and London, 2004), chapter 16.

9. A. Woolf, "The Origins and Ancestry of Somerled: Gofraid mac Fergusa and 'The Annals of the Four Masters,'" *Mediaeval Scandinavia* 15 (2005), 199–213 at 211.

10. Woolf, "Origins and Ancestry of Somerled," 211.

11. "Ceannaigh Duain t'Athar, a Aonghas (Pay For Your Father's Poem, Aonghas)," in *Duanaire na Sracaire. Songbook of the Pillagers: Anthology of Scotland's Gaelic verse to 1600*, eds. W. McLeod and M. Bateman, trans. M. Bateman (Edinburgh, 2007), 80–90.

12. Woolf, "Origins and Ancestry of Somerled," 199–213, at 212–213.

13. G.W.S. Barrow, *Kingship and Unity: Scotland 1000–1300*, 2nd ed. (Edinburgh, 2003), chapter 7.

14. On Alexander II's policies towards Argyll and the Isles see N. Murray "Swerving from the Path of Justice: Alexander II's Relations with Argyll and the Western Isles, 1214–1249," in R. Oram (ed.), *The Reign of Alexander II, 1214–49* (Leiden and Boston, 2005), 285–305.

15. See, for example, D. Alexander, T. Neighbour, and R. Oram, "Glorious Victory? The Battle of Largs, 2 October 1263," *History Scotland* 2, no. 2 (March/April 2002), 17–22.

16. On these events see E.J. Cowan, "Norwegian Sunset—Scottish Dawn: Hakon IV and Alexander III," in N. Reid (ed.), *Scotland in the Reign of Alexander III 1249–1286* (Edinburgh, 1990), 103–131; E.J. Cowan, "The Last Kings of Man, 1229–1265," in S. Duffy and H. Mytum (eds.), *New History of the Isle of Man Volume III: The Medieval Period 1000–1406* (Liverpool, 2015), 97–117; and McDonald, *Kingdom of the Isles*, chapter 4. On the Treaty of Perth see R. Lustig, "The Treaty of Perth: A Re-examination," *Scottish Historical Review* 58 (1979), 35–57.

17. *Annals of Furness* in *Chronicles of the Reigns of Stephen, Henry II and Richard I*, ed. R. Howlett, 4 vols. (London, 1884–1889), ii, 549; the annals were probably produced more or less contemporaneously and preserve original information from 1260 to 1298: See the introduction to *Chron. Stephen*, ii, lcccviii–lxxxix.

18. Barrow, *Kingship and Unity: Scotland 1000–1300*, chapter 7.

19. N. Reid, "Alexander III: The Historiography of a Myth," in N. Reid (ed.), *Scotland in the Reign of Alexander III 1249–1286* (Edinburgh, 1990), 181–213.

20. *CRMI*, f. 47r.

21. E.J. Cowan, "Norwegian Sunset—Scottish Dawn," 107–110. King Hakon IV had recently annexed Iceland, bringing an end to the era of the Icelandic commonwealth, so as an Icelander, Sturla was probably sympathetic to the plight of the Hebridean chieftains. On Sturla see now J.V. Sigurðsson and S. Jakobsson (eds.), *Sturla Þórðarson: Skald, chieftain and Lawman* (Leiden and Boston, 2017).

22. *Hakon's Saga*, trans. Dasent, 270; see the discussion in Reid, "Alexander III: The Historiography of a Myth," 184.

23. *Hakon's Saga*, trans. Dasent, 270.

24. *Hakon's Saga*, trans. Dasent, 248.

25. Cowan, "Norwegian Sunset—Scottish Dawn," 106–107.

26. *CRMI*, f. 49v.

27. *CRMI*, f. 50r.

28. *Chronicon de Lanercost*, ed. J. Stevenson (Edinburgh, 1839), 97–98; translated in *Early Sources of Scottish History, A.D. 500–1286*, ed. and trans. A.O. Anderson, 2 vols. (Edinburgh, 1922, repr. Stamford, 1990), ii, 672–673.

29. There must be a certain irony in the fact that the death of Alexander III in 1286 generated verses, preserved in the early fifteenth-century *Chronicle* of Andrew of Wyntoun, lamenting "Our golde was changit in to lede" and asking Christ to "Succoure Scotland, and ramede/That stade is in perplexite": *The Triumph Tree: Scotland's Earliest Poetry AD 550–1350*, trans. T.O. Clancy (Edinburgh, 1998), 297; discussion in C. Jones, "*Inclinit to Diuersiteis*: Wyntoun's Song on the Death of Alexander III and the 'Origins' of Scots Vernacular Poetry," *Review of English Studies* New Series 64 no. 263 (2013), 21–38.

30. C. Edwards, "Thomas of Erceldoune [called Thomas the Rhymer] (fl. late 13th cent.), Supposed Author of Poetry and Prophecies," *Oxford Dictionary of National Biography*, 2006. 22 August 2018. http://www.oxforddnb.com/view/10.1093/ref:odnb/9780198614128.001.0001/odnb-9780198614128-e-8833

31. *Scotichronicon by Walter Bower in Latin and English*, gen ed. D.E.R. Watt, 9 vols. (Aberdeen, 1987–1997), vol. 5, bk. X, chapter 44, 428–429.

32. *The Acts of Alexander III King of Scots 1249–1286*, ed. C. J. Neville and G. G. Simpson. Regesta Regum Scottorum IV Part I. (Edinburgh, 2012), no. 171; C. McNamee, "The Isle of Man under Scottish Rule, 1266–1333," in S. Duffy and H. Mytum (eds.), *New History of the Isle of Man, Volume III: The Medieval Period 1000–1406* (Liverpool, 2015), 121.

33. The *Lanercost chronicle* names four bailies: Godred MacMares, Alan fitz Count, Maurice Okarefair (or Akarsan) and Reginald the King's Chaplain: *Lanercost*, 64.

34. *Annals of Furness* in *Chronicles of the reigns of Stephen*, ii, 570–571; trans. *Scottish Annals from English chroniclers, A.D. 500–1286*, ed. and trans. A.O. Anderson (London, 1908; repr. Stamford, 1991), 382–383.

35. McDonald, *Manx Kingship*, 102–107; G. Broderick, "Irish and Welsh Strands in the Genealogy of Godred Crovan," *Journal of the Manx Museum* 8 (1980), 32–38.

36. *Annals of Furness* in *Chronicles of the Reigns of Stephen*, ii, 570–571; trans. *Scottish Annals from English Chroniclers*, ed. and trans. Anderson, 382–383. Further discussion in McDonald, *Sea Kings*, epilogue.

37. *Foedera, conventiones, litterae, et cujuscunque generis acta publica, inter reges Angliae et alios quosvis imperatores, reges, pontifices, principes, vel com-*

munitates habita aut tractata, ed. T. Rymer, 10 vols. (Hagae Comitis, 1739–1745), i, pt. iii, 74; *Monumenta de Insula Manniae, or a Collection of National Documents Relating to the Isle of Man*, ed. and trans. J.R. Oliver, 3 vols. (Douglas, 1860–1862), ii, 110–111.

38. *The Register of the Priory of St. Bees*, ed. J. Wilson (Durham, 1915), no. 497, 489.
39. See C. McNamee, "The Isle of Man under Scottish Rule, 1266–1333," 118–150.
40. *CRMI*, f. 50r.
41. See C. McNamee, "The Isle of Man under Scottish Rule, 1266–1333," 118–150.

BIBLIOGRAPHY

The Acts of Alexander III King of Scots 1249–1286. 2012. Edited by C.J. Neville and G.G. Simpson. Regesta Regum Scottorum IV Part I. Edinburgh.

Alexander, D., T. Neighbour, and R. Oram. 2002. Glorious Victory? The Battle of Largs, 2 October 1263. *History Scotland* 2 (2): 17–22.

Barrow, G.W.S. 2003. *Kingship and Unity: Scotland AD 1000–1300*. 2nd ed. Edinburgh.

Broderick, G. 1980. Irish and Welsh Strands in the Geneaology of Godred Crovan. *Journal of the Manx Museum* 8: 32–38.

Chronicles of the Reigns of Stephen, Henry II and Richard I. 1884–1889. Edited by R. Howlett, 4 vols. London.

Chronicon de Lanercost. 1839. Edited by J. Stevenson. Edinburgh.

Cowan, E.J. 1990. Norwegian Sunset—Scottish Dawn: Hakon IV and Alexander III. In *Scotland in the Reign of Alexander III 1249–1286*, ed. N. Reid, 103–131. Edinburgh.

———. 2015. The Last Kings of Man, 1229–1265. In *New History of the Isle of Man Volume III: The Medieval Period 1000–1406*, ed. S. Duffy and H. Mytum, 97–117. Liverpool.

Cronica Regum Mannie & Insularum. Chronicles of the Kings of Man and the Isles BL Cotton Julius A vii. 1995. Edited by G. Broderick, 2nd ed. Douglas; repr. 1996; 1st ed., 1979.

Duanaire na Sracaire. Songbook of the Pillagers: Anthology of Scotland's Gaelic verse to 1600. 2007. Edited by W. McLeod and M. Bateman and translated by M. Bateman. Edinburgh.

Early Sources of Scottish History, A.D. 500–1286. 1922. Edited and translated by A.O. Anderson, 2 vols. Edinburgh; repr. Stamford, 1990.

Edwards, C. 2006. Thomas of Erceldoune [called Thomas the Rhymer] (fl. late 13th cent.), Supposed Author of Poetry and Prophecies. *Oxford Dictionary of National Biography*. August 22, 2018. http://www.oxforddnb.com/

view/10.1093/ref:odnb/9780198614128.001.0001/odnb-97801986
14128-e-8833

Foedera, conventiones, litterae, et cujuscunque generis acta publica, inter reges Angliae et alios quosvis imperatores, reges, pontifices, principes, vel communitates habita aut tractata. 1739–1745. Edited by T. Rymer, 10 vols. Hagae Comitis.

Hákonar saga Hákonarsonar. 2013. Edited by Þ. Hauksson, S. Jakobsson, and T. Ulset, 2 vols. Reykjavík.

Highland Papers. 1914–1934. Edited by J.R.N. MacPhail, 4 vols. Edinburgh.

Jones, C. 2013. *Inclinit to Diuersiteis:* Wyntoun's Song on the Death of Alexander III and the 'Origins' of Scots Vernacular Poetry. *Review of English Studies* New Series 64 (263): 21–38.

Lustig, R. 1979. The Treaty of Perth: A Re-examination. *Scottish Historical Review* 58: 35–57.

MacPhee, K. 2004. *Somerled: Hammer of the Norse.* Castle Douglas.

McDonald, R.A. 1997. *The Kingdom of the Isles: Scotland's Western Seaboard, c. 1100–c. 1336.* East Linton.

———. 2007. *Manx Kingship in Its Irish Sea Setting 1187–1229: King Rognvaldr and the Crovan Dynasty.* Dublin.

———. 2015. Man, Somerled, and the Isles: The Rise of a New Dynasty. In *New History of the Isle of Man, Volume III: The Medieval Period 1000–1406,* ed. S. Duffy and H. Mytum, 58–78. Liverpool.

———. 2019. *The Sea Kings: The Late Norse Kingdoms of Man and the Isles, c. 1066–1275.* Edinburgh.

McNamee, C. 2015. The Isle of Man under Scottish Rule, 1266–1333. In *New History of the Isle of Man, Volume III: The Medieval Period 1000–1406,* ed. S. Duffy and H. Mytum, 118–150. Liverpool.

Monumenta de Insula Manniae, or a Collection of National Documents Relating to the Isle of Man. 1860–1862. Edited and translated by J.R. Oliver, 3 vols. Douglas.

Murray, N. 2005. Swerving from the Path of Justice: Alexander II's Relations with Argyll and the Western Isles, 1214–1249. In *The Reign of Alexander II, 1214–49,* ed. R. Oram, 289–305. Leiden and Boston.

The Register of the Priory of St. Bees. 1915. Edited by J. Wilson. Durham.

Reid, N. 1990. Alexander III: The Historiography of a Myth. In *Scotland in the Reign of Alexander III 1249–1286,* ed. N. Reid, 181–213. Edinburgh.

The Saga of Hakon, and a Fragment of the Saga of Magnus, with Appendices. 1894. Translated by Sir G.W. Dasent. *Icelandic Sagas and Other Historical Documents Relating to the Settlements and Descents of the Northmen on the British Isles,* vol. 4. London.

Scotichronicon by Walter Bower in Latin and English. 1987–1997. Gen Edited by D.E.R. Watt, 9 vols. Aberdeen.

Scottish Annals from English Chroniclers, A.D. 500–1286. 1908. Edited and translated by A.O. Anderson, London; repr. Stamford 1991.

Sellar, W.D.H. 2000. Hebridean Sea Kings: The Successors of Somerled, 1164–1316. In *Alba: Celtic Scotland in the Medieval Era*, ed. E.J. Cowan and R.A. McDonald, 187–218. East Linton.

Stokes, W., trans. and ed. 1897. The Annals of Tigernach. *Revue Celtique* 18: 9–59, 150–303 at 195; Electronic Version Online at CELT: Corpus of Electronic Texts: A Project of University College Cork, College Road, Cork, Ireland (2010) at http://www.ucc.ie/celt/published/T100002A/index.html

Sturla Þórðarson: Skald, chieftain and Lawman. 2017. Edited by J.V. Sigurðsson and S. Jakobsson. Leiden and Boston.

Sykes, B. 2004. *Adam's Curse: A Future Without Men*. New York and London.

———. 2006. *The Blood of the Isles: Exploring the Genetic Roots of Our Tribal History*. London.

The Triumph Tree: Scotland's Earliest Poetry AD 550–1350. 1998. Translated by T.O. Clancy. Edinburgh.

Woolf, A. 2005. The Origins and Ancestry of Somerled: Gofraid mac Fergusa and 'The Annals of the Four Masters'. *Mediaeval Scandinavia* 15: 199–213.

CHAPTER 5

Manxmen and Saints: Local Heroes in the *Chronicles of the Kings of Man and the Isles*

Abstract The Manx kings descended from Godred Crovan form the principal focus of the *Chronicles*, but they are not the only heroes to be found within its folios. The group described by the *Chronicles* as the "Manx race" or else more simply "Manxmen" plays prominent roles serving the best interests of the Manx community, particularly at times of crisis. The Isle of Man also possessed other protectors in the form of the saints, the supernatural powers of whom form the subject of three significant episodes in the text. The roles assumed by both groups of local heroes illuminate hitherto neglected aspects of identity within the Kingdoms of Man and the Isles.

Keywords *Chronicles of the Kings of Man and the Isles* • Manxmen • Manx identity • Manx community • Saints • Miracles • St. Machutus (Maughold)

To recap so far: I have argued that the principal focus of the *Chronicles* is upon the Manx sea kings descended from Godred Crovan, and that these kings naturally enough take centre stage in the account of the text. From this point of view it is therefore permissible to regard them as the "heroes" of the chronicles. Similarly, it is natural that rival dynasties or usurpers are regarded less than favourably and can be regarded as "villains"; Somerled and his descendants are regarded as causing the downfall of the Kingdom

© The Author(s) 2019   45
R. A. McDonald, *Kings, Usurpers, and Concubines in the* Chronicles
of the Kings of Man and the Isles,
https://doi.org/10.1007/978-3-030-22026-6_5

of the Isles for splitting it into two halves, and the Scottish kings Alexander II and III, the latter of whom subjugated the Isle of Man in the decade following the death of Magnus Olafsson in 1265, causing resentment and bitterness, are also regarded less than favourably. However, the matter is more complex than this, and digging more deeply into the *Chronicles* leads to further important insights.

5.1   The Manx People

If the Manx kings descended from Godred Crovan form the principal focus of the *Chronicles* and emerge as its main heroes, they are not the only heroes to be found within its folios. One of these is both surprising and communal: what the *Chronicles* refer to as the "Manx race" [*mannica gens*] (s.a. 1275) or else more simply, "Manxmen" [*Mannensibus*]. As Susan Reynolds observes, "A kingdom was never thought of merely as the territory which happened to be ruled by a king. It comprised and corresponded to a 'people' (*gens, natio,* and *populus*), which was assumed to be a natural, inherited community of tradition, custom, law and descent."[1] Given the importance of the concept of a "people" or "nation" to medieval identity, these references to the Manx people or nation are significant and worthy of reflection.

There are some 27 references to "Manxmen" throughout chronicle (and here I do not count references to "*populo Mannie*" of which there are six or seven.) The first occurs in 1079 when Godred Crovan came to Man and fought with the Manxmen (*pugnavit cum mannensibus*), and three more instances of the term occur in the same entry. In 1164 the *Chronicles* record a battle between King Godred's brother Reginald (Rognvald) and the Manxmen in which the latter were defeated. In 1172 Reginald son of Echmarcach, whose identity is uncertain, came to Man with a large force but was defeated by the Manxmen. Following the death of King Godred in 1187, the Manxmen sent ambassadors to his son Rognvald in the Isles and asked him to assume the kinship instead of his other son, Olaf. In 1224 Rognvald set out with Manxmen for the Isles to reunite the Kingdom. The same entry records the anger of the Manxmen at news that Rognvald planned to marry his daughter to Alan of Galloway, and so they sent for Olaf and made him king instead. In 1242, when King Harald arrived in the Isle of Man after being ratified in the kingship by King Hakon of Norway, he was received kindly by the Manxmen. In 1250 the Manxmen were angered by the arrogance of Ewen son of Duncan when he presumed to style himself King of the Isles; this led to conflict between the Manxmen and Ewen. In 1252 Magnus son of Olaf "came again to Man and all the Manxmen received him gladly and made him their king."[2] We may note, too, that in its account of the events of the year 1229 which saw the final acts in the long struggle between the brothers Reginald and Olaf the chronicle makes a distinction between Manx in the southern part of the island and those in the north; those in the south seem to have supported Rognvald, while those in the north seem to have favoured Olaf. This apparent distinction mirrors the longstanding and important historical distinction in the Island between the Northside and the Southside; it is evident from as early as 1079, when Godred Crovan granted the southern part of the island to the Islesmen who had supported his invasion and allotted the northern half to the native Manx.[3]

It is noteworthy that the compilers of the *Chronicles* make a clear distinction between Manxmen and Islesmen. In 1224, for instance, the Manxmen were said not to be disposed to fighting Olaf or the Islesmen, and a distinction is drawn again in the context of Harald's reign, in 1237 and in 1242. More significant perhaps is the prominent role played by a group described by the chronicle in several places as the "chieftains of the Isles" (*principes insularum*). This is the group who sent for Olaf, son of Godred Crovan, following the turbulent events of 1095–1103/1113, and similarly in 1153 it was the chieftains of the Isles who elected Godred Olafsson as king following his return from Norway. In 1224 Olaf received hostages from the chieftains of the Isles as part of his struggle with his brother. It is possible to attach names to some of these chieftains of the Isles as, for example, in 1154, when Thorfin son of Ottar requested that Somerled send his son Dugald to be king in the Isles, and when another chieftain named Paul son of Boke informed Olaf Godredsson of the plot being hatched against him by King Rognvald's wife and son in 1223. Similarly, a miracle story placed by the chronicle in 1250 relates the adventures of "a certain chieftain called Donald, a man of great age and a nobleman whom Harald, Olaf's son, considered worthier than the rest."[4] Although the identities of these individuals remain murky, it is noteworthy that the *Chronicles* sometimes offers a brief, almost formulaic, comment on their position or status. Thus, for instance, Paul son of Boke is described as "a man of vigour and power in all the Kingdom of the Isles," while Thorfin son of Ottar is said to have been "more powerful than the rest."[5]

These references are of interest for several reasons. One striking feature of the references to Manxmen in the *Chronicles* is their prominence in times of crisis, acting in what might be termed the best interests of the Kingdom. We see the "Manxmen" acting not only as defenders of the realm from external threats (as, perhaps ironically, in 1079, against Godred Crovan; in 1164 against Reginald brother of Godred; in 1172 against Reginald son of Echmarcach; and in 1250 against Ewen son of Duncan), but also at crucial moments in the succession, as happened on the death of Godred in 1187. The justification for this intervention is clearly and significantly articulated in the *Chronicles*:

> But when Godred died the Manxmen sent their ambassadors to the Isles to summon Reginald, since he was a sturdy man and of maturer [sic] years, and they made him their king. They were worried about Olaf's weakness, as he was only ten years old, and they thought that, one who did not know how to look after himself on account of the tenderness of his age would be quite unable to govern a people subject to him. This was why the Manx people established Reginald as their king.[6]

Similarly, despite what may appear as the propensity of Manx dynasts to perpetrate violence against one another in the folios of the text (more below), we also see instances in which the "Manxmen" act in such circumstances, sometimes in an attempt to bring an end to internecine feuding, as we are told occurred in 1224:

> The following year Reginald set out with Manxmen for the Isles, taking with him Alan, Lord of Galloway, to get back from Olaf part of the territory he had given his brother and to subject it again to his dominion. But because the Manxmen were not disposed to fighting Olaf or the Islesmen, as they held them in esteem, Reginald and Alan ... achieved nothing and returned home. A short time after Reginald ... set out for the court of Alan, Lord of Galloway. On that occasion he gave his daughter to Alan's son in matrimony. When the Manxmen heard about this, they were extremely angry, and sending for Olaf they made him their king.[7]

The subject of medieval Manx identity remains largely, if not entirely, unexplored, but these references in the *Chronicles* surely provide food for thought, suggesting, as they do, that a sense of identity existed within the Kingdom. Of course, since the eleventh to mid-thirteenth century material in the *Chronicles* was written only in the late 1250s we cannot be certain about the extent to which such an identity actually existed from the late eleventh century, as opposed to the extent to which it is projected backwards by the scribe writing in the 1250s—on balance, the latter seems perhaps more likely. However, since other neighbouring realms including both England and Scotland had well-developed senses of identity by the second half of the thirteenth century, it does not seem unlikely that similar developments were taking place in the contemporary Kingdom of Man and the Isles.

Given the manner in which this identity is often associated with the best interests of the Kingdom and often exercised at moments of crisis, can we in fact perhaps posit the existence of a Manx community of the realm?[8] Considering that the late thirteenth century was a key period in the development of this concept in both Scotland and England, this may not be going too far. Indeed, it is interesting and surely significant that a letter of the inhabitants of Isle of Man to Edward I in 1290 makes reference to "all people, inhabiting the Isle of Man" [*omnes homines, Insulam de Man inhabitantes*] and includes a reference at the end of the document to their "common seal" [*sigillum nostrum commune*].[9] This reference to a common seal is perhaps surprising and is seldom remarked upon in a Manx context. Yet it must surely call to mind the precisely contemporary seal utilized by the Scottish guardians during the period 1286–1292 which famously bore the legend "*Andrea Scotis dux esto compatriotis*" ("Andrew be leader of the compatriot Scots") and has been frequently discussed within the context of Scottish identity and the community of the realm of Scotland.[10] As a final observation on the topic it is worth noting that a letter of King Edward III of England to his Justiciar of Ireland relating to mercantile activity in 1343 contains a reference to the "community of the Isle of Man" (*Communitatis Insulae de Man*), although this takes us well beyond the period of the Kingdom of Man and the Isles.[11]

5.2 Supernatural Heroes: Saints

The group identified by the *Chronicles* as Manxmen was not the only one looking out for the best interests of the Manx community. The Isle of Man also possessed other protectors in the form of the saints, the supernatural powers of whom form the subject of three interesting and important episodes in the text.

The first of these concerns Magnus Barelegs, king of Norway (d. 1103), whose expedition to the Southern Isles in 1098 is documented in the *Chronicles* as well as several Old Norse Icelandic manuscripts.[12] The Manx chronicle relates how King Magnus wished to determine whether the body of St. Olaf (d. 1030) was incorrupt and gave orders that his tomb (at Trondheim cathedral) should be opened. Despite the opposition of the clergy the king had the shrine opened nevertheless, and the chronicle says that when he saw that the body was indeed intact a great fear came over him, followed that night by St Olaf appearing to him in a dream, telling him that he should either leave Norway or lose his life and Kingdom within 30 days. King Magnus of course chose to leave Norway and this is presented as the cause of his expedition to the Isles. It is interesting to note that the *Chronicles* is the only source to preserve this supernatural account of the cause of the expedition, which is variously attributed to a desire to reassert Norwegian hegemony in the region or else to a desire to take revenge for the death of Harald Sigurdarson, Magnus's grandfather, in his ill-fated invasion of England in September of 1066.[13]

The second miracle follows the *Chronicles'* account of events in 1156 and 1158 and the flight of King Godred into exile to Norway. It is introduced with the comment that, "It is permissible to insert here [an account of] a certain miracle about St. Machutus, a confessor of the Lord."[14] The *Chronicles* then relate how, when Somerled was at Ramsey, it was "reported to his army that the church of St. Machutus was packed with a lot of moveable property."[15] This is of course a reference to Kirk Maughold in the north of the Island, not far from Ramsey; as discussed below, it was a major ecclesiastical centre. One of Somerled's chieftains, named Gilcolm, brought this to Somerled's attention and urged the looting of the monastery, but Somerled, while he granted Gilcolm permission to loot, declined to participate himself. Gilcolm ordered his supporters to prepare to attack at first light; in the meantime, when word of the impending attack reached the church, it "struck everyone with such fear that many of the people who were there fled from the church, and hid themselves in caves and in the secret places of rocks. The rest of the crowd with continual cries implored God's mercy the whole night long through the merits of St. Machutus." The saint was moved to intervention, and, appearing before Gilcolm in his tent, clad in a white toga and holding a shepherd's staff, "raised up the staff which he held in his hand and drove its point through his (Gilcolm's) heart." Twice more St. Machutus stabbed Gilcolm through the heart with the point of his staff, and when the stricken chieftain's cries roused his followers they found him near death, seeking pardon for his intended bad deeds against the church. Clerics were summoned, but refused to pardon Gilcolm, with the result that, "in great pain and torment he expired about the sixth hour of the day." Somerled and his army fled in terror: "Somerled and his army were so terror-stricken by his death that, as soon as the tide was in and their ships afloat, they took the fleet out of that port."[16]

The third and final miracle is situated near the end of the text. It relates how, during the struggles for the kingship that followed the drowning of King Harald in 1248, a chieftain named Donald, described as "a man of great age and a nobleman whom Harald, Olaf's son, considered worthier than the rest,"[17] was persecuted by Harald, the son of Godred Don, and imprisoned on "a certain island situated in the wood at Myroscough where he was put under heavy guard." The chronicle continues:

> ...Now the aforesaid chieftain had great faith in the Lord. Whenever he could he would get down on his knees to the Lord and pray that he should free him from his bonds through the intervention of His mother the blessed Virgin Mary, from whose monastery he had been treacherously seized. Divine help did not fail him, for one day while he was sitting in his cell with only two guards ... suddenly the chain dropped off his feet and provided him with a free opportunity to escape.[18]

Following his successful escape Donald fled to Rushen Abbey, and the account of the miracle concludes with the remark that, "This we have written just as we have learned it from his own mouth," an important insight into the value of oral tradition in the compilation of the *Chronicles*.[19]

Modern scholarship has long since moved away from attempting to evaluate the veracity of miracles like these. Instead, scholars now seek to understand and explain the roles and functions served by saints and miracles in medieval society—to understand these things within the context of medieval society, as it were, rather than to assess them according to modern scientific standards of evidence. Approached in this way, instead of being dismissed as evidence of superstition, credulity, or ignorance, saints and miracles have been shown to have served many significant roles in medieval society. In the early middle ages saints often acted as supernatural protectors or avengers of their monasteries, lands, and those dedicated to them, and this aspect is evident in all three of the miracles preserved in the *Chronicles*. It is particularly pronounced, however, in the miracle attributed to St. Machutus, where Machutus—a local saint—acts as a protector of his monastery and local people in the face of an external enemy who sought to violate the monastery. The violence of the miracle and the slaying of the chieftain Gilcolm might surprise us, but in fact this type of miracle is quite common in early medieval miracle stories and collections, where saints often wreak retribution upon those who would injure their followers.[20] The miracles of St. Faith of Conques, for example, collected by the early eleventh-century scholar Bernard of Angers (fl. c. 1010–1020), have been extensively studied, and are described by one modern authority as "miracles for the protection of the monks, the extension of their lands, and the aggrandisement of their church through their saint ... St Faith is seen as the protector of her own people, as great a lord as any in the countryside."[21]

The miracles also serve to illuminate something of the broader picture of devotion and dedication in the Isle of Man. St. Machutus or Maughold was a local saint (albeit an obscure one) and the monastery dedicated to him in the north of the Island, not far from Ramsey, was an important early Christian foundation in the Island that survived and thrived into the twelfth century at least.[22] But the twelfth century was also noted for the establishment of the reformed religious order of the late eleventh and early twelfth century in the Isle of Man—religious orders that originated on the Continent and were "alien" to the Island, being imported by the Manx kings like Olaf who founded Rushen Abbey c. 1134. These included important new Continental orders such as the Augustinians, Savignacs, and Cistercians.[23] Even though the account of the *Chronicles* was composed in the late 1250s, it is interesting that the story is predicated upon a flourishing ecclesiastical centre at Maughold in the middle of the previous century. The *Life of St. Patrick* composed by Jocelin (fl. 1175–1214) Abbot of Furness Abbey in Lancashire c. 1185, which contains important information on St. Machutus in the early middle ages, also contains a brief but important reference to the church of St. Maughold in the twelfth century.[24] This squares with archaeological evidence, and several of the carved stones date from the era of the Crovan kings. Two of them, carved with runic inscriptions by "John the priest," date from around 1200 and probably relate to processes of parish formation in the Island.[25] The list of bishops appended to the Manx chronicle informs us that Bishop Hrólfr, the first of the Manx bishops recorded by the chronicle, of whom little is known, was buried here: "The first bishop before Godred Crovan began to rule was Hrólfr, who lies at St. Maughold's Church."[26] One of the largest of the inscribed stones at the site is known as Roolwer's stone,[27] suggesting the importance of the place around the end of the eleventh century. It is also worth noting that the inclusion of the miracle of St. Machutus within the chronicle demonstrates that the monks of Rushen Abbey maintained interests in the hagiographical traditions of the Island; indeed, the account may be derived from a now-lost hagiographical text.[28]

If St. Machutus represents what we might regard an early medieval saint associated with the conversion of the Island, the Blessed Virgin Mary, on the other hand was one of the "international" Biblical saints that gained prominence across Europe from the late eleventh century. The spread of the cult of the Blessed Virgin Mary was aided in part by the centralized devotion of the Cistercian order which required all monasteries to be dedicated to the Virgin Mary—and we note this aspect in the chronicle's account of Donald which concludes, fittingly enough, with the information that the chieftain returned to the monastery dedicated to Mary at Rushen Abbey.[29] Thus, the miracle stories in the *Chronicles* provide an illuminating cross-section of religious devotion in the Isle of Man in the twelfth and thirteenth centuries, which appears as an intriguing mix of old and new that mirrors the broader changes taking place in religious and especially monastic life across the British Isles in the same period.[30]

There is, however, another facet to the miracle stories, and one which links them to the broader topic of kingship in the *Chronicles*. This is because each miracle is inserted at a particular point in the text at which there is a comment to be made about kingship. The miracle concerning St. Olaf and Magnus Barelegs, although it's probably the most difficult of the three to comprehend in this regard, seems to show King Magnus in a poor light and to suggest that his assumption of kingship in the Isles is essentially an intrusion and that he is therefore a usurper.[31] In support of this it may be noted that, following the death of Magnus, the chieftains of the Isles sent for Olaf son of Godred and had him installed in the kingship, thereby re-establishing the line of Godred Crovan in the kingship. The miracles concerning St. Machutus and the Blessed Virgin Mary, however, are much easier to read in terms of legitimate kingship in Man and the Isles. The miracle of St. Machutus, as noted above, illustrates the saint as protector of his church and people against an external invader: the miracle clearly casts the chieftain Gilcolm as the perpetrator of the crime, but it also seems designed to cast Somerled, as the leader of the invading forces (and, it will be recalled, as the cause of the splitting of the Kingdom), in a bad light as well. Even though Somerled states, "Let it be between you and St. Machutus. I and my army will remain blameless. We are having no part of your booty,"[32] we also note that Somerled and his men flee in terror upon the death of Gilcolm. Later, when the chronicle records the death of Somerled in an invasion of the Scottish mainland in 1164, it remarks that "by the divine vengeance he was overcome by a handful of men and killed there along with his son and a countless number of people…".[33] This seems to suggest that God was on the side of the Manx kings after all, and the anecdote fits broadly into the *Chronicles'* categorization of Somerled as a usurper and an enemy of the Manx kings discussed above.

The third and final miracle in the *Chronicles*, that in which the Blessed Virgin aids the chieftain Donald in escaping from captivity, can also be read in relation to the text's commentary on the kings of the Manx dynasty, but in order to better understand this point we need to examine several other aspects of the *Chronicles* first.

NOTES

1. S. Reynolds, *Kingdoms and Communities in Western Europe 900–1300* (Oxford, 1984), chapter 8, quote at 250. Much has been written on the topic of late, but Reynolds remains an essential starting point. The Presidential addresses of Professor R.R. Davies to the Royal Historical Society between 1993 and 1997 are also essential reading on the topic: R.R. Davies, "The Peoples of Britain and Ireland 1100–1400: I. Identities," *Transactions of the Royal Historical Society* 4 (1994), 1–20; "The Peoples of Britain and Ireland 1100–1400: II. Names, Boundaries and Regnal Solidarities," *Transactions of the Royal Historical Society* 5 (1995), 1–20; "The Peoples of Britain and Ireland 1100–1400: III. Laws and Customs," *Transactions of the Royal Historical Society* 6 (1996), 1–23; "The Peoples of Britain and Ireland 1100–1400: IV. Language and Historical Mythology," *Transactions of the Royal Historical Society* 7 (1997), 1–24.
2. *Cronica Regum Mannie & Insularum. Chronicles of the Kings of Man and the Isles BL Cotton Julius A vii*, ed. G. Broderick, 2nd ed. (Douglas, 1995; repr. 1996; 1st ed. 1979), f. 49r [hereafter *CRMI*].
3. *CRMI*, f. 33r. On this division and its significance see most recently G. Williams, "The System of Land Division and Assessment," in S. Duffy and H. Mytum (eds.), *A New History of the Isle of Man, Volume III. The Medieval Period 1000–1406* (Liverpool, 2015b), 466–483.
4. *CRMI*, f. 47v.
5. *CRMI*, f. 42v, f. 37r.
6. *CRMI*, f. 40v.
7. *CRMI*, f. 43v.
8. Antonia Gransden observes that, in a contemporary English context, "many chroniclers appealed to the right of the community of the realm to act against bad government": "The Chronicles of Medieval England and

Scotland," in *Legends, Traditions and History in Medieval England* (London and Rio Grande, 1992), 218; the point is worth noting in our context, although it should not be pressed too far.

9. *Monumenta de Insula Manniae, or a Collection of National Documents Relating to the Isle of Man*, ed. and trans. J.R. Oliver, 3 vols. (Douglas, 1860–1862), ii, 110–111.

10. G.W.S. Barrow, *Robert the Bruce and the Community of the Realm of Scotland*. 3rd ed. (Edinburgh, 1988), 16–18, 26–28; see also U. Hall, *The Cross of St. Andrew* (Edinburgh, 2006), 99–101.

11. Oliver, *Monumenta*, ii, 192–195, and see also 196–197.

12. Including *Morkinskinna: The Earliest Icelandic Chronicle of the Norwegian Kings (1030–1157)*, trans. with introduction and notes by T.M. Andersson and K.E. Gade (Ithaca and London, 2000), 285–313; *Fagrskinna: A Catalogue of the Kings of Norway*, trans. A. Finlay (Leiden, 2003); Snorri Sturluson, *Heimskringla*, trans. A. Finlay and A. Faulkes, 3 vols. (London, 2011–2015), iii, 127–144; and *Orkneyinga Saga*, see note 13 below.

13. *Orkneyinga Saga: The History of the Earls of Orkney*, trans. H. Pálsson and P. Edwards (London, 1981), 83. R. Power, "Magnus Barelegs' Expeditions to the West," *Scottish Historical Review* 73 (1985), 107–132, is a seminal treatment of the subject.

14. *CRMI*, f. 38r. According to medieval legend, Maughold (Machutus) was a pagan Irish chieftain and leader of a band of pirates who was converted by St. Patrick and set adrift in a vessel with no oars as penance for his sins. He is said to have washed ashore in the Isle of Man, where he eventually became bishop. Whatever we make of these legends (discussed in H. Birkett, *The Saints' Lives of Jocelin of Furness: Hagiography, Patronage and Ecclesiastical Politics* (Woodbridge, 2010), 42–44), the ecclesiastical settlement dedicated to him at Maughold was a prominent centre of Christianity in the Isle of Man from the seventh to the twelfth or thirteenth centuries. Jocelin's statement that the remains of an early monastery at Maughold could be seen in his own day, at the end of the twelfth century, is likely correct, and the mention of the place in the *Chronicles* is the earliest reference to it in an historical document (as opposed to Jocelin's *hagiographical* text, which is, of course, earlier.) On Maughold see A. Johnson and A. Fox, *A Guide to the Archaeological Sites of the Isle of Man up to AD 1500* (Douglas, 2017), 153–161, and P. Davey, *After the Vikings: Medieval archaeology of the Isle of Man AD 1100–1550* (Douglas, 2013), 96–99.

15. *CRMI*, f. 38r.

16. *CRMI*, f. 39r.

17. *CRMI*, f. 47v.

18. *CRMI*, f. 47v–48r.

19. *CRMI*, f. 48r.

20. See B. Ward, *Miracles and the Medieval Mind: Theory, Record and Event 1000–1215*. Rev. ed. (Philadelphia, 1987). There is also much of value in R. Finucane, *Miracles and Pilgrims. Popular Beliefs in Medieval England* (New York, 1977).
21. Ward, *Miracles*, 36–42, quote at 42; see also *The Book of Sainte Foy*, trans. with an introduction and notes by P. Sheingorn (Philadelphia, 1995).
22. See Johnson and Fox, *Guide to the Archaeological Sites of the Isle of Man*, 153–161; and P. Davey, *After the Vikings: Medieval Archaeology of the Isle of Man AD 1100–1550* (Douglas, 2013), 96–99.
23. A good introduction is J. Burton, *Monastic and Religious Orders in Britain, 1000–1300* (Cambridge, 1994); on monasticism in the Isle of Man see P.J. Davey, "Medieval Monasticism and the Isle of Man, c.1130–1540," in S. Duffy and H. Mytum (eds.), *A New History of the Isle of Man, Volume III. The Medieval Period 1000–1406* (Liverpool, 2015), 349–376.
24. See Birkett, *The Saints' Lives of Jocelin of Furness*, 44 and n. 97, and in B.R.S. Megaw, "The Monastery of St. Maughold," *Proceedings of the Isle of Man Natural History and Antiquarian Society* 5, no. 2 (1946–1950), 169–181.
25. P.M.C. Kermode, *Manx Crosses*, with an introduction by David M. Wilson (Balgavies, 1994), 212–214, pl. lxiii, lxiv; J.W. Radcliffe and C.K. Radcliffe, *A History of Kirk Maughold* (Douglas, 1979), 29–30. See now Johnson and Fox, *A Guide to the Archaeological Sites of the Isle of Man*, 153–161.
26. *CRMI*, f. 50v. The episcopal succession at this juncture is tremendously problematic, thanks to a severely patchy documentary record: see A. Woolf, "The Early History of the Diocese of Sodor," in S. Duffy and H. Mytum (eds.), *A New History of the Isle of Man, Volume III. The Medieval Period 1000–1406* (Liverpool, 2015), 329–348; and A. Woolf, "The Diocese of the Sudreyar," in S. Imsen (ed.), *Ecclesia Nidrosiensis 1153–1537* (Trondheim, 2003), 171–182.
27. Kermode, *Manx Crosses*, 142–146.
28. M.T. Flanagan, "Jocelin of Furness and the Cult of St Patrick in Twelfth-Century Ulster," in C. Downham (ed.), *Jocelin of Furness Proceedings of the 2011 Conference* (Donington, 2013), 63.
29. On the Blessed Virgin Mary see M. Warner, *Alone of All Her Sex: The Myth and the Cult of the Virgin Mary* (London, 1976), esp. chapter 8; the prominent role of the Cistercians in spreading the cult is addressed at 131. On the Cistercians see G. Coppack, *The White Monks: The Cistercians in Britain 1128–1540* (Stroud, 2000).
30. See R.A. McDonald, *Manx Kingship in Its Irish Sea Setting 1187–1229: King Rögnvaldr and the Crovan Dynasty* (Dublin, 2007), 192–200; Davey, "Medieval Monasticism and the Isle of Man," in S. Duffy and H. Mytum (eds.), *A New History of the Isle of Man, Volume III. The Medieval Period 1000–1406* (Liverpool, 2015), 349–376.

31. B. Williams, "Chronicles of the Kings of Man and the Isles," in S. Duffy and H. Mytum (eds.), *A New History of the Isle of Man, Volume III. The Medieval Period 1000–1406* (Liverpool, 2015a), 319–320.
32. *CRMI*, f. 38r.
33. *CRMI*, f. 39r.

BIBLIOGRAPHY

Barrow, G.W.S. 1988. *Robert the Bruce and the Community of the Realm of Scotland*. 3rd ed. Edinburgh.

Birkett, H. 2010. *The Saints' Lives of Jocelin of Furness: Hagiography, Patronage and Ecclesiastical Politics*. Woodbridge.

The Book of Sainte Foy. 1995. Translated with an introduction and notes by P. Sheingorn. Philadelphia.

Burton, J. 1994. *Monastic and Religious Orders in Britain, 1000–1300*. Cambridge.

Coppack, G. 2000. *The White Monks: The Cistercians in Britain 1128–1540*. Stroud.

Cronica Regum Mannie & Insularum. Chronicles of the Kings of Man and the Isles BL Cotton Julius A vii. 1995. Edited by G. Broderick, vii–xvi, 2nd ed. Douglas; repr. 1996; 1st ed. 1979.

Davey, P. 2013. *After the Vikings: Medieval Archaeology of the Isle of Man AD 1100–1550*. Douglas.

Davey, P.J. 2015. Medieval Monasticism and the Isle of Man, c. 1130–1540. In *A New History of the Isle of Man, Volume III. The Medieval Period 1000–1406*, ed. S. Duffy and H. Mytum, 349–376. Liverpool.

Davies, R.R. 1994. The Peoples of Britain and Ireland 1100–1400: I. Identities. *Transactions of the Royal Historical Society* 4: 1–20.

———. 1995. The Peoples of Britain and Ireland 1100–1400: II. Names, Boundaries and Regnal Solidarities. *Transactions of the Royal Historical Society* 5: 1–20.

———. 1996. The Peoples of Britain and Ireland 1100–1400: III. Laws and Customs. *Transactions of the Royal Historical Society* 6: 1–23.

———. 1997. The Peoples of Britain and Ireland 1100–1400: IV. Language and Historical Mythology. *Transactions of the Royal Historical Society* 7: 1–24.

Fagrskinna: A Catalogue of the Kings of Norway. 2003. Translated by A. Finlay. Leiden.

Finucane, R. 1977. *Miracles and Pilgrims. Popular Beliefs in Medieval England*. New York.

Flanagan, M.T. 2013. Jocelin of Furness and the Cult of St Patrick in Twelfth-Century Ulster. In *Jocelin of Furness: Proceedings of the 2011 Conference*, ed. C. Downham, 45–66. Donington.

Gransden, A. 1992. The Chronicles of Medieval England and Scotland. In *Legends, Traditions and History in Medieval England*, 199–238. London and Rio Grande.

Hall, U. 2006. *The Cross of St. Andrew*. Edinburgh.

Johnson, A., and A. Fox. 2017. *A Guide to the Archaeological Sites of the Isle of Man up to AD 1500*. Douglas.

Kermode, P.M.C. 1994. *Manx Crosses*, with an introduction by David M. Wilson. Balgavies.

McDonald, R.A. 2007. *Manx Kingship in its Irish Sea Setting 1187–1229: King Rögnvaldr and the Crovan Dynasty*. Dublin.

Megaw, B.R.S. 1946–1950. The Monastery of St. Maughold. *Proceedings of the Isle of Man Natural History and Antiquarian Society* 5: 169–181.

Monumenta de Insula Manniae, or a Collection of National Documents Relating to the Isle of Man. 1860–1862. Edited and translated by J.R. Oliver, 3 vols. Douglas.

Morkinskinna: The Earliest Icelandic Chronicle of the Norwegian Kings (1030–1157). 2000. Translated with introduction and notes by T.M. Andersson and K.E. Gade. Ithaca and London.

Orkneyinga Saga: The History of the Earls of Orkney. 1981. Translated by H. Pálsson and P. Edwards. London.

Power, R. 1985. Magnus Barelegs' Expeditions to the West. *Scottish Historical Review* 73: 107–132.

Radcliffe, J.W., and C.K. Radcliffe. 1979. *A History of Kirk Maughold*. Douglas.

Reynolds, S. 1984. *Kingdoms and Communities in Western Europe 900–1300*. Oxford.

Sturluson, Snorri. 2011–2015. *Heimskringla*. Translated by A. Finlay and A. Faulkes, 3 vols. London.

Ward, B. 1987. *Miracles and the Medieval Mind: Theory, Record and Event 1000–1215*. Rev. ed. Philadelphia.

Warner, M. 1976. *Alone of All Her Sex: The Myth and the Cult of the Virgin Mary*. London.

Williams, B. 2015a. The Chronicles of the Kings of Man and the Isles. In *New History of the Isle of Man Volume III: The Medieval Period 1000–1406*, ed. S. Duffy and H. Mytum, 305–328. Liverpool.

Williams, G. 2015b. The System of Land Division and Assessment. In *A New History of the Isle of Man, Volume III. The Medieval Period 1000–1406*, ed. S. Duffy and H. Mytum, 466–483. Liverpool.

Woolf, A. 2003. The Diocese of the Sudreyar. In *Ecclesia Nidrosiensis 1153–1537*, ed. S. Imsen, 171–182. Trondheim.

———. 2015. The Early History of the Diocese of Sodor. In *A New History of the Isle of Man, Volume III. The Medieval Period 1000–1406*, ed. S. Duffy and H. Mytum, 329–348. Liverpool.

CHAPTER 6

Women, Marriage and Kin-Feud in the *Chronicles of the Kings of Man and the Isles*

Abstract Women are few and far between in the folios of the *Chronicles*, yet a close reading of the text reveals that they play key roles. Women's roles as wives, mothers, and inciters are crucial to understanding some of the central themes of the text concerning matrimonial politics, kingship, kin-strife, and what the compiler of the Chronicle lamented as "the cause of the collapse of the entire Kingdom of the Isles". These strands are realized in the Chronicle's account of the "deeds of the brothers Reginald and Olaf," with its detailed and dramatic narrative of the kin-feud between the brothers that spanned four decades of Manx and Hebridean history and shaped the remaining history of the dynasty.

Keywords Women • Marriage • Concubinage • Queens of the Isles • Kin-feud • Family • Succession

It is a striking fact that the *Chronicles*, like many such sources of the medieval period, are overwhelmingly male-dominated.[1] Women are few and far between in its folios, yet a close reading of the text will reveal that women play key roles. In fact, the roles of women as wives, mothers, and inciters are crucial to understanding some of the central themes of the text concerning succession politics, kin-strife, and what the compiler of the *Chronicles* lamented as "the cause of the collapse of the entire Kingdom of the Isles."[2] Thus, as Susan M. Johns has argued in a contemporary

© The Author(s) 2019   59
R. A. McDonald, *Kings, Usurpers, and Concubines in the* Chronicles
of the Kings of Man and the Isles,
https://doi.org/10.1007/978-3-030-22026-6_6

medieval Welsh context, "placing women and gender at the heart of the analysis raises new questions about the construction of history."[3]

6.1   WOMEN IN THE *CHRONICLES*

Excluding brief mentions about foreign rulers (such as the death of St Margaret of Scotland in 1093 or that of Queen Margaret of Scotland, sister of King Edward I of England, in 1274[4]), only five women are named in a Manx context in the *Chronicles*. They are:

- Affrica, the daughter of Fergus (d. 1161), the ruler of Galloway in southwest Scotland, married King Olaf Godredsson (d. 1153). Their son was Godred Olafsson (d. 1187). The Chronicle also says that Olaf "had many concubines from whom he begat three sons, namely Reginald, Lagman and Harald, and many daughters, one of whom married Somerled, ruler of Argyll." [5]
- Fionnula [Finnguala] is described as "a daughter to MacLochlann, son of Muircheartach King of Ireland, and mother of Olaf [Godredsson]"; she was probably the daughter of Niall Mac Lochlainn, king of Cenél nEógain in the north of Ireland (1170–1176).[6] Her marriage to King Godred Olafsson (d. 1187), which is discussed in detail further below, is crucial to our story.
- Affrica, the daughter of King Godred Olafsson (d. 1187). She married John de Courcy (d.c. 1219), the Anglo-Norman conqueror of Ulster, probably around 1180 (though the date is nowhere firmly recorded).[7] Relatively little is unfortunately known of Affrica herself, but the marriage of a member of the Manx dynasty to an Anglo-Norman adventurer represents an important manifestation of the manner in which Manx interests in Ireland were radically reoriented in the decades following the English invasion of Ireland.[8]
- Lauon, described as the "daughter of a certain nobleman of Kintyre," married Olaf Godredsson (d. 1237) around 1223. She was the sister of King Rognvald's own wife (who is not named—and more on her in a moment).[9] The fact that the *Chronicles* do not name her father is an intriguing little puzzle. This may be explicable in the context of the castigation of the descendants of Somerled as usurpers and "villains" by the chronicle, however. Since the MacSorleys were the dominant family in Kintyre around the time of the events described, it is possible that Lauon's father was a member of this rival kindred,

perhaps Ruaidri the son of Ranald (Raghnall) the son of Somerled, and his name, accordingly, may have been excluded from the record for reasons of partisanship already noted.[10] On the other hand, this is far from certain (our understanding of landholding in Kintyre in the thirteenth century is vague at best[11]), and it is also possible that the chronicler simply did not know the name of her father.

- Christina, the daughter of Earl Ferchar of Ross in Scotland (d.c. 1251). Ferchar was a significant figure in the north-west highlands of Scotland and one closely aligned with the Scottish king Alexander II (r. 1214–1249).[12] Christina married Olaf Godredsson (d. 1237) after the bishop of the Isles declared Olaf's marriage to Lauon uncanonical; it was annulled, and he subsequently married Christina. It is an intriguing question as to whether Harald (d. 1248) was Olaf's son by Lauon or Christina. The *Chronicles* states that he was fourteen years old when he began to rule in 1237; if correct, this would place his birth right around the tumultuous events of 1223 and would allow the possibility that he was the son of either Lauon or Christina. Given the manner in which Olaf's marriage with Lauon seems to have been regarded as uncanonical, however, it seems difficult to imagine that Harald could have escaped censure had Lauon been his mother. Still, the issue is an intriguing one, and it is interesting that the chronicle does not make an explicit statement about his maternity—particularly when it *does* make an explicit statement about the maternity of another ruler, King Olaf Godredsson (d. 1237).[13]

There are also several other, unnamed, women in the *Chronicles* in a Manx context:

- King Rognvald's wife, Lauon's sister, is described as "queen of the Isles" (*regina Insularum*). She is mentioned twice and named on neither occasion and the reference to her as *regina Insularum* is unique in the Manx chronicle (and nearly unique in the history of the dynasty![14]). She is alleged to have incited the renewal of strife between the brothers Rognvald and Olaf—as the chronicle puts it, she "sowed the seeds of all the disharmony between Reginald and Olaf."[15] She is said to have done this around 1223 (see further below) by sending a letter in King Rognvald's name to his son Godred in the Isle of Skye, to the effect that Godred should seize and kill Olaf. Her role in inciting the strife between Rognvald and Olaf is likely the reason she is nameless in the *Chronicles*, a crucial point to which we shall return below.

- Finally, there is a daughter of King Rognvald, who also is unnamed. She seems to have been married to, or else was intended to be married to, the son of Alan the Lord of Galloway (d. 1234) as part of the political intrigues that marked the tumultuous conclusion to Rognvald's reign.[16] This marriage, whether it actually took place or not, was the spark that led to Rognvald's expulsion by the Manx and to the eventual victory of Olaf in struggle with his brother.[17]

Striking as it may be to the modern reader, there is nothing surprising in the gender imbalance and the treatment of women throughout the Manx chronicle. Medieval society, as is well known, was generally misogynistic, not least because most texts were produced in ecclesiastical environments, and, according to church doctrine, women were responsible for original sin. Most medieval texts therefore come with a certain amount of gender bias and, often, misogyny, built right into them. [18] Bearing in mind that the chronicle was produced in just such a context—Rushen Abbey, a Cistercian house—it is only natural that it shares the general values and biases of the time.

Appreciating the gender bias of the text, it is possible to make some observations on women and their roles in the chronicle. Above all, we see the importance of marriage and marriage alliances in medieval politics. One of the key roles of aristocratic women in medieval society was as pawns on the chessboard of medieval politics, where marriage alliances forged bonds between members of the ruling elite.[19] The Manx chronicle seems particularly concerned—one is tempted to say obsessed—with what might be termed "legitimate" as opposed to "illegitimate" marriages and unions. In medieval societies, and particularly in and around the Irish Sea Basin, not all marriages were equal. In particular, the theme of polygyny, a form of polygamy in which a man had a principal, official wife and one or sometimes even more secondary wives or concubines, appears throughout the text.[20] King Olaf Godredsson's (d. 1153) practice of keeping concubines was remarked upon, for instance, and the chronicler states that it was the marriage of one of his daughters by a concubine to Somerled that brought about the downfall of Kingdom of the Isles. The chronicle speaks well of Olaf except when discussing his matrimonial politics and practice of keeping of concubines: "he was devout and enthusiastic in matters of religion…except that he over-indulged in the domestic vice of kings."[21] Despite the regularization of King Godred's (d. 1187) marriage by the papal legate in 1176, the practice evidently continued into the early thirteenth century: his son, King Olaf Godredsson (d. 1237), is said to have kept a concubine prior to his marriage to Lavon—a cousin of that lady, in fact.[22]

There was, of course, nothing unusual in this behaviour, which was practiced in many contemporary societies in Ireland, Wales, Scotland, the Hebrides, Norway, and elsewhere. Somerled himself, said by the *Chronicles* to have married a daughter of King Olaf and to have had four children by her, is reputed in later Gaelic tradition to have had additional children from other unions, possibly born to concubines or the result of other marriages.[23] However, such customs increasingly came under fire from the Church reformers of the eleventh and twelfth century, who regarded them, in the words of one modern scholar, as "outlandish, barbaric and utterly corrupt."[24] In 1073–1074, for example, Lanfranc, archbishop of Canterbury (d. 1089), famous for his reforming zeal, wrote to two Irish rulers, criticizing, among other things, the sexual laxity of the Irish. In a letter to Toirrdelbach Ua Briain, king of Munster (d. 1086), Lanfranc observed that, "in your kingdom a man abandons at his own discretion and without any grounds in canon law the wife who is lawfully married to him, not hesitating to form a criminal alliance—by the law of marriage or rather by the law of fornication—with any other woman he pleases, either a relative of his own or of his deserted wife or a woman whom someone else has abandoned in an equally disgraceful way." The Ostman king of Dublin, Guthric, received a similarly venomous letter from the archbishop.[25] The struggle for reform was very much an uphill one, however, and secular marriage persisted into the seventeenth century in Gaelic Ireland, Scotland, and elsewhere.[26] Similar complaints were registered by reformers about the matrimonial and sexual situation in Wales. The churchman and scholar Gerald of Wales (Giraldus Cambrensis, d.c. 1223), writing in the 1190s, listed incest, trial marriage, and inheritance by illegitimate sons among the less praiseworthy characteristics of the Welsh people,[27] although it appears that native matrimonial customs did not persist in Wales to the same degree that they did in Ireland and Scotland.[28]

These changing attitudes towards concubinage and illegitimate children are clearly evident in the folios of the *Chronicles*. We have already noted, for instance, the text's condemnation of King Olaf for keeping concubines, and this attitude is shared in the account of the annulment of

Olaf Godredsson's marriage by Reginald, the bishop of the Isles. An important turning point appears to have been a visit to the Isle of Man by the papal legate Cardinal Vivian in 1176–1177, during which Vivian "caused king Godred to be lawfully betrothed to his wife called Fionnula [Finnguala], a daughter to MacLochlann, son of Muircheartach king of Ireland, and mother of Olaf who was then three years old."[29] The Cardinal's Irish Sea itinerary is attested in other contemporary sources, where he is said to have embarked from Whithorn in Galloway for the Isle of Man on 24 December 1176, and to have made a brief sojourn in the Island before departing on 6 January for Ireland, where he arrived to find himself in the thick of John de Courcy's conquest of the Ulaid.[30]

6.2   RIGHTFUL KINGS, USURPERS, AND KIN-FEUD
IN THE CHRONICLES

One of the major dynastic problems arising from the practice of polygyny could be a proliferation of sons by women of differing social status: as Robin Frame colourfully summed it up: "virile, long-lived kings left behind them a galaxy of sons, born of women of varying origins and status."[31] This fact is not only evident throughout the pages of the *Chronicles*, but also simultaneously provides the key to unlocking the central message of the text. This is because the text is about not simply the dynasty of Manx sea kings descended from Godred Crovan: it also represents an attempt to justify or legitimize one line of kings of that dynasty—that descended from Olaf Godredsson (d. 1237)—over another, rival line— that descended from Olaf's brother, King Rognvald Godredsson (d. 1229). This returns us to the theme of succession politics and kin-feud within the *Chronicles*, and in particular to the titanic struggle between the brothers Rognvald and Olaf for the kingship that spanned several decades from the late 1180s to the end of the 1220s. As I hope to demonstrate, the feud between the brothers is tied directly to questions of gender and power.

Even a casual perusal of the *Chronicles* reveals that power did not pass smoothly through the line of Godred Crovan, with the result that the kingship was often contested by members of the royal kindred. This is evident from virtually the beginning of the dynasty, when, following the death of Godred Crovan in 1095, the kingship was contested among these three sons, Lagman, Harald, and Olaf. Lagman, the eldest, seized power, but was challenged by his brother Harald, who, the chronicle says, "rebelled against him for a good while." Harald was ultimately captured and mutilated by blinding and castration—an action of which his brother Lagman so repented that he is said to have gone on pilgrimage to Jerusalem, dying en route. Following Lagman's death (or perhaps even before it, if unrest began while he was on pilgrimage), Irish, Norwegian, Manx, and insular powers competed for dominance for at least a decade, culminating in the famous western expedition of King Magnus Barelegs of Norway in 1098. The chronology of this period is almost hopelessly confused, and it was not until about 1113 that Olaf Godredsson was established in the kingship of Man and the Isles. Olaf is said by the *Chronicles* to have reigned for 40 years (an exceptional reign-length for the period), but a new round of internecine strife characterized the final years of his rule. The *Chronicles* relates how, in 1152, three of Olaf's nephews, the sons of his brother Harald, who had been raised at Dublin, "collected together a huge throng of men and all the exiles of the king, and came to Man demanding that half the entire Kingdom of the Isles be given to them."[32] At a subsequent meeting at Ramsey, Olaf was treacherously killed by one of his nephews:

> On the appointed day both parties convened at the port called Ramsey; they sat in rows, the king with his men on one side, the conspirators with their men on the other. Reginald, the middle brother, who was to strike him [Olaf], was standing apart talking to one of the chieftains of the land. When he was summoned he came to the king, and turning himself towards him as though to salute him he raised his gleaming axe into the air and with one blow cut off the king's head.[33]

The three brothers then divided the Isle of Man amongst themselves and launched an attack on Galloway. The next autumn, in 1153, Olaf's son Godred, who had been in Norway at the time of his father's death, returned with Norwegian backing. The Manx elected him to the kingship, and he promptly extracted revenge for his father's killing by slaying one of the killers and blinding the others.[34]

Worse was to come, however. In fact, the most intensive period of internecine rivalry in the history of the entire dynasty was that between the brothers Rognvald and Olaf that spanned most of Rognvald's reign (1187–1229). In the Manx chronicle, approximately eight folios (of its total of 39) cover the period between the death of Godred Olafsson in

1187 and that of Rognvald in 1229. Of those, about six—that is, nearly 15 per cent of the total length of the chronicle, but nearly all of the space devoted to Rognvald's reign—are concerned with the conflict between Rognvald and Olaf, inserted following the notice of the death of Bishop Nicholas in 1217 and forming a coherent block down to Rognvald's death in 1229. The chronicler begins: "For the benefit of the readers it is considered not out of place now to relate briefly something about the deeds of the brothers Reginald and Olaf,"[35] and I believe that this narrative device is utilized here with the intent of highlighting the significance of the episode within the text.[36]

The framework for the struggle was laid in the reign of King Godred Olafsson (r. 1154–1187). Godred—perhaps in an attempt to stabilize the succession following his own experience in 1153/1154—had made provision, while still alive, that his son Olaf should succeed him, since he was said to have been "born in lawful wedlock" (more on that in a moment). The *Chronicles* relates, however, that the Manx instead chose Rognvald as their king since, "he was a sturdy man and of maturer years," and Olaf was said to have been only ten years of age. Upon taking the kingship, Rognvald granted his brother the island of Lewis in the Outer Hebrides, where Olaf lived, we are told, "leading a poor sort of life."[37] When Olaf approached Rognvald for a larger share of the Kingdom, Rognvald had him arrested and sent to King William I of Scotland (1165–1214), who imprisoned him; this would, incidentally, place the period of his captivity between about 1207 and late 1214 or early 1215, as William died on 4 December 1214.[38] Following his release, Olaf is said to have undertaken a pilgrimage to Santiago de Compostella, from which he returned an undisclosed time later to be received peaceably by Rognvald, who then prevailed upon his brother to marry the daughter of a "certain nobleman from Kintyre" named Lauon, the sister to Rognvald's own wife. Olaf was again granted the Isle of Lewis and went off to live there. Not long after Olaf had settled in Lewis, however, Reginald, the bishop of the Isles (d.c. 1226) undertook a visitation of the churches, and informed Olaf that his recently contracted marriage was illicit, because Olaf had previously been married to the first cousin of his wife. Bishop Reginald assembled a synod and annulled the marriage between Olaf and Lauon; Olaf then wedded Christina, the daughter of Ferchar Maccintsacairt, either already, or soon to be, styled earl of Ross, a significant figure in the north-west highlands of Scotland and one closely aligned with the Scottish king Alexander II (1214–1249).[39]

These events so angered Rognvald's wife, Lauon's sister, that she, in the words of the chronicler, "sowed the seeds of all the disharmony between Reginald and Olaf."[40] She did this, we are told, by sending a letter secretly under King Rognvald's seal to his son Godred in the Isle of Skye, instructing him to kill Olaf. Godred duly collected an army and went to Lewis, where Olaf eluded him and escaped in a small boat to the court of his father-in-law in Ross. Godred devastated Lewis, killed a few men, and returned home. Meantime, a disaffected official, Paul, son of Boke, described as "sheriff [vicecomes] of Skye and a man of vigour and power in all the kingdom of the Isles" defected from Godred, "as he was not willing to agree to Olaf's murder." Paul joined Olaf in exile in Ross where he and Olaf entered into a pact of friendship and alliance. Olaf and Paul returned to Skye, gathered support, and ambushed Godred at a "certain island called the isle of St. Columba."[41] (This has sometimes been interpreted as Iona, but the Chronicle's description of the site suggests rather that it either was tiny Skeabost Island on the Isle of Skye, a few hundred metres above the mouth of the River Snizort, within which are the remains of a churchyard and several structures including a church dedicated to St Columba, or *Eilean Chaluim Chille* in Kilmuir, which until the eighteenth century lay in the middle of the now drained Loch Chaluim Chille.[42]) Whatever the location, Godred's supporters were cut down and he himself was taken, blinded, and castrated. Olaf, we are told, did not agree with this action, and the chronicle explicitly places the blame on Paul, son of Boke. This episode is stated by the *Chronicles* to have taken place in the year 1223, and Icelandic annals for the same year also record this turn of events.[43]

The turning of the tables on Godred by Olaf and Paul foreshadowed the final reversal of Rognvald's own fortunes. Though he had held the upper hand in the struggle with his brother up to 1223, the wheel of fortune was evidently turning. The next year, 1224, Olaf gained the advantage when he came to Man and landed at Ronaldsway with a fleet of 32 ships. The *Chronicles* relate that: "Reginald and Olaf divided the kingdom of the Isles between themselves. Man was given to Reginald in addition to his share with the title of king. Olaf then received provisions from the people of Man and returned with his host to his share of the Isles."[44]

By 1226, Rognvald found himself ousted entirely, living in exile at the court of Alan, Lord of Galloway (d. 1234). The final acts of the decades-old feud were played out in the winter of 1228–1229. A punitive invasion of the Isle of Man by Alan and Rognvald was repelled by Olaf, and so a second invasion was orchestrated in January 1229 in which Rognvald attacked and burned Olaf's ships at Peel and managed to gain enough support in the island to force a showdown with his brother. On the four-teenth day of February, the feast of St Valentine the Martyr, the two brothers with their respective armies met at Tynwald, the ancient assembly-centre for the annual *Þing* and the ceremonial heart of the Island. The meeting of the brothers near this important site suggests that a parley or negotiation may have been intended, although the outcome was a battle in which Rognvald's army was "put to flight like sheep." Rognvald himself was cut down on the spot; the Manx chronicle hinted that treachery was involved.[45] We are told that Olaf was greatly perturbed by the death of his brother, "however he did not in his lifetime vindicate his death."[46] The implications of treachery in the death of Rognvald are echoed in other sources that relate the event; the *Chronicle of Lanercost*, possibly using a source cognate with the Manx chronicle, remarked that, "Reginald, the king of the islands, fell a victim to the arms of the wicked."[47]

Despite the death of Rognvald and the accession of Olaf to the Kingdom, the feud between them cast long shadows across the next 30 years of Manx and Hebridean history. One of the consequences of the struggle between Rognvald and Olaf and the ensuing instability in the Isles was the awakening of a slumbering giant in the person of King Hakon IV of Norway (r. 1217–1263). In the winter of 1228/1229, greatly con-cerned by reports of the turmoil stirred up the feud between Rognvald and Olaf, he ordered the outfitting of a fleet to go west across the sea and restore order, and appointed its command to an obscure individual named Uspak (probably a descendant of Somerled), giving him both the royal name Hakon and the title of king in the Islands.[48] Of particular signifi-cance here is the fact that, according to the version of events presented in the Manx chronicle, not only did Olaf join the expedition, but so too did Rognvald's son, Godred Don.[49]

Godred's reappearance on the scene following his mutilation at the hands of Olaf's ally Paul son of Boke on the Isle of Skye in 1223, the last he is heard of in the Chronicle, comes as something of a surprise. It is an open question as to whether or not this is the same Godred son of Rognvald mentioned in 1223, despite the introduction of the Gaelic sobriquet "Don," (*donn*) "Brown, or brown-haired,"[50] at this juncture in the *Chronicles*; I am inclined to believe it is, although it is perhaps just pos-sible that Rognvald had two sons named Godred, one of whom was slain in 1223 and one of whom, known as Godred "Don," resumed the struggle in 1230.[51] Whatever the case, the presence of a son of Rognvald evidently reopened the question of competition for the kingship. It seems at least possible that King Hakon had ordered a partition of the Kingdom between Olaf and Godred; in any event this is precisely what happened when the fleet reached Man in 1230, in the wake of an assault on the island of Bute (then under Scottish control) and the subsequent death of Uspak.[52]

The situation, predictably, did not last. The *Manx chronicle* and *Hákonar Saga* together relate an epic tale of intrigue, conflict, and revenge. The Chronicle relates how Godred set out for the Isles, "but was killed in the island called Lewis;" neither his killer nor the circumstances of his demise are explained.[53] Following his death, however, Olaf reigned unchallenged until his own death in 1237. The *Saga of Hákon*, however, adds further interesting details. Not only is it stated that Paul son of Boke was among the leaders of the Norwegian expedition of 1230, but Paul and Olaf sailed on the same warship, suggesting that the old alliance of 1223 had endured.[54] The saga goes on to relate how Paul "fell a few weeks afterwards at the hands of Godred the Black, the son of King Rognvald."[55] Taken together, the Manx chronicle and the *Saga of Hákon* seem to reveal the culmination of the feud between Rognvald and Olaf, played out by Rognvald's son and his allies in the Hebrides a year or so after the fall of Rognvald himself. What can be inferred from the chronicle and the saga at this point is the mutual annihilation of the two men, Paul, son of Boke, evidently still allied with Olaf, and Godred determined to win revenge not only for his father's killing but also, perhaps, for his own mutilation some seven years earlier. The Chronicle states that Godred was slain on Lewis, while the saga gives only the "Southern Isles" as the location. Regardless, it was evidently only after the demise of Godred Rognvaldsson that Olaf was secure in his tenure of the kingship. He ruled for seven more years, down to his own death in 1237, and was buried in St Mary's Abbey at Rushen.[56]

After Olaf's death, his fourteen-year-old son, Harald, succeeded him. His reign was certainly not without troubles, but dynastic challenges do not seem to have been among them. Factional strife erupted on Man in the wake of Harald's departure for the Isles soon after his succession; it does not appear to be linked to the feuding of the previous generation, but the account in the chronicle is far from explicit.[57] Then, in 1238, Harald was expelled from the Kingdom by envoys from the Norwegian king, "because he refused to go to the court of the king of Norway."[58] Only in 1242, having spent several years in Norway, was Harald restored to the kingship. "And so from that time on," says the Manx chronicle, "he began ruling quietly and peacefully in Man."[59] Harald was drowned in a shipwreck off Sumburgh head in Shetland en route from Norway to Man in the autumn of 1248,[60] and his death ignited a new, final round of dynastic struggle in Man and the Isles that defined the years 1249 to 1254.

The Manx chronicle relates how, following Harald's death, his brother Reginald succeeded to the kingship and began reigning on 6 May 1249. He was, however, slain soon thereafter by a knight called Ivar (*Yuaro milite*) near Rushen on 30 May in circumstances that remain far from clear.[61] The identity of Ivar is far from certain and constitutes a minor mystery of Manx medieval history. Whoever Ivar was, however, he did not apparently seek the kingship for himself. The Chronicle records that, upon the death of Reginald in 1249, Harald the son of Godred Don began ruling in Man, and it therefore seems most likely that Ivar was an agent or ally of Harald. In fact, one of the witnesses to a 1246 charter of King Harald Olafsson was *domino Yuor' de Mann'*, "Lord Ivar of Man." Both the chronology and the coincidence of name mean this is almost certainly the individual responsible for the death of Reginald in May 1249, while the designation *dominus* also suggests he was a high-status individual.[62] A letter of King Henry III of England of April 1256, in which he ordered his men not to receive Harald, Ivar, or their accomplices, who "wickedly slew Reginald formerly king of Man," seems to support the notion of an alliance between Ivar and Harald, and seems to cement an identification of the killer of Reginald with the Lord Ivar of the charter.[63]

More significantly, however, the appearance of a son of Godred Don on the scene nearly twenty years after the fall of his father reveals the continuing rivalry between the lines of Rognvald and Olaf as well as the shifting balance of power between them. The *Chronicles* certainly regarded Harald unfavourably, remarking that he "usurped the title and dignity of king in Man for himself and banished practically all the chieftains of king Harald, Olaf's son,"[64] while the approval that Olaf had apparently found is also reflected in his correspondence with the English king. As an illustration of Harald's alleged tyranny and oppression, the Chronicle inserts a lengthy story of a miracle of St Mary in favour of a chieftain named Donald who had been persecuted by Harald (his precise identity is unclear).

> There was a certain chieftain called Donald, a man of great age and a nobleman whom Harald, Olaf's son, considered worthier than the rest. Escaping the persecution of Harald, son of Godred Don, he came to the monastery

of St. Mary at Rushen with his infant son. The aforesaid Harald followed him to the monastery, but because he was unable to bring violence to bear on him in the holy place, he spoke to him in words of flattery and deceit, saying, "Why did you wish to escape in this way? I have no intention of doing you harm." He promised him safe conduct on oath and persuaded him that he could go freely wherever he wished throughout the land. The man trusted in the king's oath and good faith and followed him out of the monastery. After a while the king, following wicked counsel and even forgetful of his oath and good faith, had the aforesaid man seized and bound, and led to a certain island situated in the wood at Myroscough where he was put under heavy guard.

Because of Donald's great faith and dedication to the Blessed Virgin Mary, however, "Divine help did not fail him, for one day while he was sitting in his cell with only two guards … suddenly the chain dropped off his feet and provided him with a free opportunity to escape…"[65] The miracle, which can now be properly understood within its context in the *Chronicles*, is clearly intended to illustrate that God was on the side of the descendants of Olaf rather than of Rognvald, as is evident from its characterization of Harald son of Godred Don as an usurper and oath-breaker, and the miraculous intervention in favour of Donald, an adherent of King Harald.

When the narrative returns to its main strand, we learn that Harald was subsequently summoned to Norway in 1250 because "the king was angry with him for seizing possession of the kingdom to which he had no right…"[66] Harald was detained in Norway and is not heard from again. It is thus clear that by 1250 both English and Norwegian monarchs were choosing to recognize the Manx kings descended from Olaf Godredsson as legitimate rulers of the Kingdom, while Rognvald's descendants were increasingly marginalized and apparently regarded as usurpers, even, significantly, by the compiler of the Manx chronicle.

The next event recorded by the chronicle is the arrival at Man in 1250 of Magnus, son of Olaf, and Ewen son of Duncan with a Norwegian fleet.[67] The aim of the expedition is far from clear, but it appears to have been the installation of Magnus as king. As noted above, things did not go smoothly, and Ewen's apparent arrogance as well as his claiming of the title of king for himself resulted in conflict. It was not until 1252 that Magnus was finally established in Man in 1252, where we are told that, "all the Manxmen received him gladly and made him their king."[68] Magnus subsequently travelled to Norway, where he was established in the kingship with Norwegian protection. The chronicle adds the interesting detail that "His opponents got to see and hear of this and became alarmed, but, their hopes (of supplanting him) dashed, they gradually faded away"[69]—suggesting that even as late as the middle of the 1250s there were those who preferred the claims of Harald, son of Godred Don; certainly Henry III's 1256 letter of protection for Magnus reads as though Harald and Ivar were still alive, perhaps, as the account of the Manx chronicle suggests, in Norway. Magnus, however, reigned unchallenged until his death in 1265, which also marked the end of the dynasty.

What, then, can be said about these struggles within the royal family of Man and the Isles? To begin, we may note, simply, both their prevalence in the text and within the dynasty as a whole. Beginning in the generation after Godred Crovan and continuing down to the time of the last Manx king, they literally span the entire history of the dynasty. No generation was free of the spectre of internecine strife. Another particularly striking aspect of the internecine struggles within the Crovan dynasty is their savage and bloody nature. In the struggle for power among the sons of Godred Crovan, Harald, who challenged Lagman, was eventually blinded and castrated. King Olaf Godredsson was publicly decapitated by one of his nephews in 1153; Olaf's son, Godred, eliminated the murderers of his father by killing one and mutilating two others. In 1164 the brother of Godred named Rognvald suffered mutilation at the hands of Godred. Given the bloody backdrop to the rivalry for kingship within the kindred of Godred Crovan, Rognvald's treatment of his brother Olaf may seem mild by comparison, though this did not prevent Rognvald from falling in battle in circumstances which medieval chroniclers implied were treacherous. Moreover, as part of the struggle between the brothers Rognvald and Olaf, Rognvald's son Godred Don was mutilated by blinding and castration in 1223, and was killed in Lewis around 1230. Twenty years later, in May 1249, the shadowy figure named Ivar assassinated Reginald Olafsson, who had just taken the kingship as the successor to the drowned Harald Olafsson. The identity of Ivar and motives for the killing remain uncertain, but there is a strong suspicion that Ivar was an associate of Harald, the son of Godred Don, who subsequently took the kingship in 1249. In the course of a century-and-a-half of rivalry among kinsmen for the kingship (1095–1250), then, a significant proportion of Manx dynasts perished by mutilation or assassination.[70] David Carpenter's description of the Manx dynasty as "highly factionalized" therefore seems entirely justified, and the frequent and violent struggles over the kingship have been regarded as representing perhaps the dynasty's greatest weakness.[71]

Of course, the treatment of high status rivals for the kingship in Man and the Isles was by no means unique within a broader British context. Dynastic struggles in twelfth-century Wales, Scotland, and Ireland frequently ended in a similar bloodbath, with rivals suffering killing or maiming. Writing about the situation in Wales following the death of a ruler, Gerald of Wales (Giraldus Cambrensis) observed that, "The most frightful disturbances occur in their territories as a result [of the death of a ruler], people being murdered, brothers killing each other and even putting each other's eyes out, for as everyone knows from experience it is very difficult to settle disputes of this sort."[72] Similar conduct existed in Scotland, as when, for instance, a struggle between the two brothers Uhtred and Gilbert of Galloway, the sons of Fergus (d. 1161), resulted in Uhtred having his eyes and tongue cut out, being castrated, and left for dead after an assault by his brother in 1175.[73] In the far north, the ongoing and often violent struggle between the Scottish king William I (r. 1165–1214) and Jarl Harald Maddadsson of Orkney/Caithness in the years around 1200 resulted in some equally bloody episodes that included the blinding of Jarl Harald's son by the king of Scots, and the severe mutilation of John, bishop of Caithness, by Harald himself.[74] John Gillingham, a leading scholar of the subject, has drawn the conclusion that, "rivalry among kinsmen for kingship was so intense that the killing and blinding of rivals remained well within the rules of acceptable conduct."[75] In Wales and Scotland, although not Gaelic Ireland, this situation had changed by the thirteenth century, as political values became increasingly "anglicized" and carried out according to rules of chivalric compassion, which spared life and limb of high status opponents and which had been transplanted to England by its French-speaking élite post 1066 and diffused throughout Wales and Scotland by the mid-thirteenth century.[76]

Such chivalric values are little in evidence among the kindred of Godred Crovan in the twelfth and thirteenth centuries, however. This might be explained by the fact that there was no direct Anglo-Norman settlement in the Isle of Man, and therefore no Anglo-Norman nobility to assimilate such behaviour. Yet the lack of Anglo-Norman settlement in Man clearly did not preclude the adoption of knighthood by members of the Crovan kindred and the Manx élite by the middle of the thirteenth century: most of the thirteenth-century Manx kings were knighted. The fact that the English kings knighted them shows very clearly the direction from which this particular set of foreign influences entered Manx society.[77] If the folios of the *Chronicles* are to be believed, then, the very interesting situation prevailed in Man whereby knighthood and, presumably, as part of its ethos, contemporary conventions of behaviour towards high-status rivals, were known, yet such conventions were also apparently ignored or over-ridden where kin-strife was concerned.

A second point is that an important consequence of kin-strife within royal kindreds was the potential for fragmentation of the Kingdom or principality in question,[78] and a striking aspect of the chronicle's accounts of feuding within the dynasty is the manner in which the kingship could be partitioned. An early and peaceful division may in fact have been made in the lifetime of Godred Crovan himself. Godred's son Lagman, who is a shadowy figure and whose reign is murky at best, is described as having been alive and in the northern Hebrides at the time of Magnus Barelegs' royal cruise in 1098. Snorri Sturluson informs us, in the saga of Magnus contained within his massive collection of Norwegian kings' sagas (*Heimskringla*), that, "Lagman was set to defend the land in the northern islands (Norðreyjum)."[79] The early thirteenth-century collection of Norse kings' sagas known as *Morkinskinna* ("rotten parchment," the name given to both the manuscript and the book) contains verses attributed to the poet Gísl Illugason (who is thought to have been a participant in King Magnus's campaign) stating that Lagman was captured off Skye, and styling him, "prince of Uist" (Ívistar gram).[80] Whether or not we consider the Kingdom to have been partitioned in the reign of Godred Crovan himself, it is clear that divisions did sometimes arise among his successors; more often than not, these were the result of feuding. Following the killing of Olaf Godredsson in 1153, for example, his nephews are said to have divided the Isle of Man amongst themselves, though whether this extended to the Hebridean possessions is unclear.[81] The years 1156 to 1158 wit-nessed the splitting of the Kingdom between Godred Olafsson and his kinsman and rival Somerled of Argyll.[82] The Manx kings retained Man and northern Hebrides but Somerled and his descendants claimed many of the Inner Hebrides; for a brief period of time from 1158 to 1164 Somerled completely evicted Godred from the kingship and ruled throughout the length and breadth of the Isles, likely including Man.[83]

The partitioning of the Kingdom between the Manx kings and the MacSorleys is significant because it endured down until the end of Kingdom of Man and Isles in 1265/1266, and meant that when the domain of the Manx kings was subsequently partitioned between feuding dynasts of the Crovan dynasty, the territory that was being divided was already truncated from that which had been controlled before the Somerledian ascendancy. Important periods of partition within the Manx dynasty occurred between Rognvald and Olaf, from about 1187 until 1226 and again, briefly, in early 1229, but there also seems to have been a later split between Olaf and Rognvald's son Godred Don in 1230. The Manx chronicle explicitly states that Olaf obtained Man and Godred seems to have been given the Isles, including Lewis, where he is said to have been slain. The next king, Harald Olafsson, seems to have ruled over an intact Kingdom, but it is really not clear what happened between his death in 1249 and the installation of Magnus in 1252, and this may, as we have seen, have represented yet another period of partition. The rule of Magnus Olafsson over a unified Kingdom from 1252 until his death in 1265 only serves to underline the significance of divisions within the territories ruled by the descendants of Godred Crovan for nearly two centuries.

6.3   "The Deeds of the Brothers Reginald and Olaf"

As a final point to tie together the question of marriage, concubinage, and feuding, and to begin to move towards some conclusions, I would like to return for a moment to the *Chronicles'* account of the feud between the brothers Rognvald and Olaf, the sons of Godred Olafsson, and I would like to suggest that this episode is in fact the hinge around which the entire text and its central narrative of feud within the dynasty turns. There are several reasons for this. First, as I have noted above, the portion of the text detailing the feud between the brothers stands apart from the rest of the text in several regards. Not only does it represent some 15 per cent of the overall length of the text, but it is the most detailed portion of the text, is distinguished and set off from the rest of the text with the remark that "for the benefit of readers..." and it follows a tightly crafted story containing significant dramatic elements. Moreover, the placement of the episode at the central position of the text—it commences at almost precisely the half-way point of the chronicle (on f. 42v)—is likely not accidental, and may have been intended deliberately to highlight its significance to the overall story.

Second, it is noteworthy that the compiler elucidates the causes of the feud between the brothers very clearly in this section of the text—and these relate, ultimately, to marriage, concubinage, and (for the compiler of the chronicle) the evil nature of women. Quite simply, the cause of the feud is the annulment of Olaf's marriage to Lauon and his second and subsequent marriage to Christina, both of which were enforced by Bishop Reginald. Moreover, the catalyst of the feud was the actions of King Rognvald's wife, Lauon's sister, who took matters into her own hands and sent a letter under her husband's name to her son, Godred, ordering him to kill Olaf. Indeed, the chronicler remarks bluntly that "stimulated by bitterness and resentment, King Reginald's wife, Queen of the Isles, sowed the seeds of all the disharmony between Reginald and Olaf"; further judgement is evident in the characterization of these actions as the "wicked wish" of the Queen.[84] This passage also, incidentally, solves the puzzle of why Rognvald's wife is nowhere named in the *Chronicles*. This omission is certainly curious. The compiler of the chronicle cannot have been ignorant of her identity, since he knows the names of Olaf's two wives, for instance, as well as the name of King Godred's principal wife, Fionnula; not only this, but the events had happened within living memory of the inception of the chronicle in the late 1250s and it is very difficult to believe that the name of the Queen of the Isles was unknown when so many other notable women of the dynasty are named within the pages of the text. Names are important in history and literature, and this un-naming therefore has the appearance of a campaign to remove from history altogether the identity of the woman who was considered responsible for the "disharmony" between brothers that characterized the subsequent history of the dynasty: a case of medieval Manx *damnatio memoriae*, a condemnation of memory and a form of dishonour which sought to erase someone from history. If this was indeed the intent of the scribe, then his effort was successful, for, as strange as it may seem, no trace of the name of Rognvald's wife appears to survive: she was a victim of what has been described as the "propaganda and character assassination" that often accompanied contemporary succession politics.[85] Another, near-contemporary case involving the manipulation of memory pertaining to a female dynast has been discerned in the case of the Welsh prince Llywelyn ap Gruffudd (d. 1282): exploring the references to Llywelyn's mother (Senana) in contemporary and later genealogical records, J. Beverley Smith remarks that "the genealogists, who so meticulously recorded the affiliations of a multitude of other men, failed to retain a memory of the name of Llywelyn ap Gruffudd's mother."[86] Susan M. Johns suggests that this omission demonstrates the manner in which social memory could be gendered from its inception, but neither Smith nor Johns goes so far as to ascribe it to a deliberate campaign of *damnatio memoriae* as I am suggesting transpired in Man and the Isles.[87]

Finally, we may return to the important and so far unresolved question of the identity of the mothers of Rognvald and Olaf. The evidence of the *Chronicles* on this important matter is surprisingly ambivalent. They say that Godred left three sons named Rognvald, Olaf, and Ivar. Nothing more is heard of Ivar, but of Rognvald the Chronicle says that he was a robust young man in the Isles, while Olaf was a tender child residing in Man. Olaf, we are told, had been appointed in Godred's lifetime to succeed him in the kingship, "as this inheritance was his by right, for he had been born in lawful wedlock." When Godred died, however, the Manx people chose Rognvald as king, since "he was a sturdy man and of maturer years," whereas Olaf was said to have been ten years old, "and they thought that, one who did not know how to look after himself on account of the tenderness of his age would be quite unable to govern a people subject to him." This, says the scribe, "was why the Manx people established Reginald [Rognvald] as their king."[88]

Behind this apparently straightforward narrative there lurk a number of problems. The reference to Olaf having been born in lawful wedlock and the inheritance being his by right must be considered in the context of the formalization of Godred's marriage to Fionnula (mentioned above) by the Papal Legate Cardinal Vivian in 1176: if Rognvald, the elder brother, had been born *before* this, he may have been regarded as illegitimate (was the same possibly true of Ivar as well?). Olaf, however, may have been acceptable because he was born either just before or immediately following the settlement. (By the sixteenth century Manx law allowed for the legitimization of a child born a year or two before the formalization of a marriage, so this might offer one solution, if we are willing to permit the application of sixteenth-century statutes to the situation in the twelfth—admittedly something of a stretch.[89]) If Olaf had not been born until 1177 this would offer another solution and would simultaneously avoid the problem of applying later Manx statutes to a much earlier period.

Another problem relates to the identity of Rognvald's mother. While the chronicle seems to suggest that Rognvald was the son of Godred and Finnguala of Ireland who was born before the formalization of their marriage by the Cardinal legate, this is not explicitly stated—in contrast to his brother Olaf, who *is* explicitly described as Finnguala's son.[90] But was this in fact the case? Some evidence points in another direction, and so perhaps

the omission is important. In an Irish praise poem, almost certainly contemporary with the first half of his reign, King Rognvald is addressed in
two places as "macSadhbha"[91] suggesting that his mother's name was
Sadhbh—perhaps an otherwise unknown Irish concubine or wife of
Godred, but certainly not a detail that a poet would have gotten wrong.[92]
This is possible in light of the Irish connections of not only Godred but his
father Olaf as well. There is also a fragmentary letter from Rognvald's
brother Olaf to King Henry III of England, dated circa 1228, in which
Olaf describes his brother as a bastard, but does not (unfortunately!) refer
to the identity of Rognvald's mother.[93] Given the intense conflict that
existed between the two brothers over the kingship at that time and the
partisan nature of the document, this could just as easily be intended as a
slur on Rognvald's claim to the kingship as an indication that he was the
son of an irregular (from the point of view of the Church) relationship
with a concubine. In the end, no firm conclusion about the identity of
Rognvald's mother is possible, but the weight of evidence is convincing to
indicate that she was of Gaelic, likely Irish, stock. It must remain an open
question whether she was Finnguala or else the Sadhbh of the praise-
poem, although there is a strong possibility that she was the latter.[94]

If Rognvald and Olaf were sons of Godred by different mothers, this
might explain the intensity of the struggle between the two brothers, and
their apparent hatred for one another. In an early medieval context, Ian
Wood has suggested that the hatred demonstrated by one member of the
Merovingian royal family for another may be explained by the practice of
concubinage.[95] Closer to the Isle of Man in both time and space, Bart Jaski
has suggested that, in the contemporary Irish context, tensions between
half-brothers could be shaped by the political background, social status,
and reputation of their respective mothers. Jaski adds: "the sources are
silent about intrigues at court, the vying for power, the scheming behind
the scenes, the competition between queens and concubines and other
personal and political games which often form the icing on the cake in
historical writing."[96] Pauline Stafford has remarked upon the manner in
which nearly contemporary succession politics in England (mid-tenth to
mid-twelfth centuries), "produced a hotbed of gossip, intrigue, and suspicion. Issues of birth, and thus of marriage, are frequently aired, especially
at a time when reforming ecclesiastical views are focusing attention on the
definition of marriage itself. Women, as the wives and mothers of claim-
ants, are natural targets…"[97] The possibility that such considerations
shaped not merely the relations between Olaf and Rognvald but also the

subsequent history of the Manx dynasty down to its extinction, is an intriguing, but ultimately perhaps insoluble, one. Whatever the case, inserting questions of gender and power into the succession politics of the Manx dynasty may provide new insights into medieval Manx and Hebridean history as well as historical writing and the manipulation of memory in the late Norse Kingdoms of Man and the Isles.

NOTES

1. See for example M. Bull, *Thinking Medieval: An Introduction to the Study of the Middle Ages* (Basingstoke, 2005), 77.
2. *Cronica Regum Mannie & Insularum. Chronicles of the Kings of Man and the Isles BL Cotton Julius A vii*, ed. G. Broderick, 2nd ed. (Douglas, 1995; repr. 1996; 1st ed. 1979), f. 35v [hereafter *CRMI*]; the term "succession politics" is used by P. Stafford, "The Portrayal of Royal Women in England, Mid-tenth to Mid-twelfth Centuries," in J.C. Parsons (ed.), *Medieval Queenship* (New York, 1996), 145–146.
3. S.M. Johns, *Gender Nation and Conquest in the High Middle Ages: Nest of Deheubarth* (Manchester, 2013), 229.
4. *CRMI*, f. 33v, f. 49v.
5. *CRMI*, f. 35v.
6. *CRMI*, f. 40r; F.X. Martin, "John, Lord of Ireland, 1185–1216," in A. Cosgrove (ed.), *New History of Ireland, Volume II: Medieval Ireland, 1169–1534* (Oxford, 1987), 135.
7. *CRMI*, f. 41r; Giraldus Cambrensis (Gerald of Wales), *Expugnatio Hibernica. The Conquest of Ireland*, ed. and trans. A.B. Scott and F.X. Martin (Dublin, 1978), 180–181. Much has been written on De Courcy and his remarkable career: see, inter alia: S. Duffy, "The First Ulster Plantation: John de Courcy and the Men of Cumbria," in T.B. Barry, R. Frame, and K. Simms (eds.), *Colony and Frontier in Medieval Ireland: Essays Presented to J.F. Lydon* (London, 1995), 1–28; S. Flanders, *De Courcy: Anglo-Normans in Ireland, England and France in the Eleventh and Twelfth Centuries* (Dublin, 2008).
8. R.A. McDonald, *Manx Kingship in its Irish Sea setting 1187–1229: King Rognvaldr and the Crovan Dynasty* (Dublin, 2007), 125–128.
9. *CRMI*, f. 42r.
10. Insightful comments on the marriage in A. Woolf, "The Age of Sea-Kings: 900–1300," in D. Omand (ed.), *The Argyll Book* (Edinburgh, 2004), 94–109 at 107.
11. This represents a significant problem in the history of the western seaboard: see for example R.A. McDonald, *The Kingdom of the Isles: Scotland's*

Western Seaboard, c. 1100–c. 1336 (East Linton, 1997), 83–85 and Woolf, "Age of Sea-Kings: 900–1300," 105–108.

12. *CRMI*, f. 42v. Ferchar is an interesting figure in his own right: see R.A. McDonald, "Old and New in the Far North: Ferchar Maccintsacairt and the Early Earls of Ross, c.1200–74," in S. Boardman and A. Ross (eds.), *The Exercise of Power in Medieval Scotland, c. 1200–1500* (Dublin, 2003), 23–45.

13. *CRMI*, f. 40r.

14. See note 85 below.

15. *CRMI*, f. 42v.

16. *CRMI*, f. 44r.

17. Another daughter of Rognvald was married to the Prince of Gwynedd Rhodri ap Owain sometime before his death in 1195, but this is unremarked upon by the Manx chronicle: Discussion in McDonald, *Manx Kingship*, 103–105, with references.

18. See, for example, Thomas Head, "Hagiography," The Orb: The On-line Reference Book for Medieval Studies at http://www.hagiographysociety. org/wp-content/uploads/2013/03/Head_Hagiography.pdf

19. A treatment of the topic in an Irish Sea/Scottish context is R.A. McDonald, "Matrimonial Politics and Core-Periphery Interactions in Twelfth- and Early Thirteenth-Century Scotland," *Journal of Medieval History* 21 (September 1995), 227–247. Similarly, see H.B. Clarke, "The Mother's Tale," in S. Booker and C.N. Peters (eds.), *Tales of Medieval Dublin* (Dublin, 2014), 52–62.

20. See D. Ó Corráin, "Women in Early Irish Society," in M. MacCurtain and D. Ó Corráin (eds.), *Women in Irish Society: The Historical Dimension* (Dublin, 1978), 1–13; B. Jaski, "Marriage Laws in Ireland and on the Continent in the Early Middle Ages," in C. Meek and K. Simms (eds.), '*The Fragility of Her Sex'? Medieval Irish Women in their European Context* (Dublin, 1996), 16–42; A. Candon, "Power, Politics and Polygamy: Women and Marriage in late Pre-Norman Ireland," in D. Bracken and D. Ó Riain-Raedel (eds.), *Ireland and Europe in the Twelfth Century: Reform and Renewal* (Dublin, 2006), 106–127. For a Norwegian context see J. Jochens, "The Politics of Reproduction: Medieval Norwegian Kingship," *American Historical Review* 92 (1987), 327–349. An important study dealing with the early medieval period is P. Stafford, *Queens, Concubines and Dowagers: The King's Wife in the Early Middle Ages* (London, 1983), see esp. 62–79.

21. *CRMI*, f. 35v.

22. *CRMI*, f. 42r–42v.

23. McDonald, *Kingdom*, 45, 69 (with references); "History of the MacDonalds," in J.R.N. MacPhail (ed.), *Highland Papers*, vol. 1. (Edinburgh, 1914), 5–72, at 11.

24. D. Ó Corráin, "Marriage in Early Ireland," in A. Cosgrove (ed.), *Marriage in Ireland* (Dublin, 1985), 5–24 at 21.

25. *The Letters of Lanfranc Archbishop of Canterbury*, ed. and trans. H. Clover and M. Gibson (Oxford, 1979), nos. 9 (to Guthric), 10 (Toirrdelbach); no. 8 displays the concern of Pope Gregory VII with Irish marriage and sexual practices.

26. D. Ó Cróinín, *Early Medieval Ireland, 400–1200* (London, 1995), 127; W.D.H. Sellar, "Marriage, Divorce and Concubinage in Gaelic Scotland," *Transactions of the Gaelic Society of Inverness* 51 (1978–1980), 464–493 at 473.

27. Gerald of Wales, *The Journey Through Wales and The Description of Wales*, trans. with an Introduction by L. Thorpe (London, 1978), 262–264, 273.

28. H. Pryce, *Native Law and the Church in Medieval Wales* (Oxford, 1993), chapter 4; see also R.R. Davies, "The Status of Women and the Practice of Marriage in Late-Medieval Wales," in D. Jenkins and M. Owen (eds.), *The Welsh Law of Women* (Cardiff, 1980), 93–114, esp. at 106–108, which deals for the most part with the later medieval period.

29. *CRMI*, f. 40r.

30. Giraldus Cambrensis (Gerald of Wales), *Expugnatio*, 174–175, 180–181 and notes on 332–333; P.C. Ferguson, *Medieval Papal Representatives in Scotland: Legates, Nuncios, and Judges-Delegate, 1125–1286* (Edinburgh, 1997), 53–55.

31. R. Frame, *The Political Development of the British Isles, 1100–1400* (Oxford, 1990), 112.

32. *CRMI*, f. 36r.

33. *CRMI*, f. 36v.

34. *CRMI*, f. 36v.

35. *CRMI*, f. 41v.

36. McDonald, *Manx Kingship*, 98–99.

37. *CRMI*, f. 41v. Although the statement has been taken as a factually accurate representation of the economic situation in the Outer Hebrides in the period, there is abundant evidence that the region was more productive than has been thought: see discussion in R. Oram and P. Adderley, "Innse Gall: Culture and Environment on a Norse Frontier in the Western Isles," in S. Imsen (ed.), *The Norwegian Domination and the Norse World c.1100–c.1400* (Trondheim, 2010), 125–148; N. Sharples and R. Smith. "Norse Settlement in the Western Isles," in A. Woolf (ed.), *Scandinavian Scotland—Twenty Years After: The Proceedings of a Day Conference held on 19 February 2007* (St. Andrews, 2009), 103–130; and McDonald, *The Sea Kings* (Edinburgh, 2019), chapter 8. This statement in the *Chronicles* might therefore represent another subtle manifestation of propaganda in the text.

38. *Early Sources of Scottish History, A.D. 500–1286*, ed. and trans. A.O. Anderson, 2 vols. (Edinburgh, 1922; repr. Stamford, 1990), ii, 398 n. 5 [hereafter *ES*].

39. McDonald, "Old and New in the Far North," 23–45.

40. *CRMI*, f. 42v.

41. *CRMI*, f. 43r.

42. R. Power, "Meeting in Norway: Norse-Gaelic Relations in the Kingdom of Man and the Isles, 1090–1270," *Saga Book* 29 (2005), 5–66 at 43, places these events in Iona. But the Manx chronicle seems clearly to indicate that they took place on Skye. On Skeabost Island see: Royal Commission on Ancient and Historical Monuments and Constructions of Scotland, *Ninth Report, With Inventory of Monuments and Constructions in the Outer Hebrides, Skye and the Small Isles* (Edinburgh, 1928), no. 616; see also A. Small, 'Norse settlement in Skye,' in R. Boyer (ed.), *Les Vikings et leur civilization. Problèmes actuels* (Paris, 1976), 29–37. W.D.H. Sellar, "The Ancestry of the Macleods Reconsidered," *Transactions of the Gaelic Society of Inverness* 60 (1997–1998), 233–258, posits Eilean Chaluim Chille in Kilmuir, and this site has been championed by S. Thomas, "From Cathedral of the Isles to Obscurity—The Archaeology and History of Skeabost Island, Snizort," *Proceedings of the Society of Antiquaries of Scotland* 144 (2014), 245–264 at 259.

43. *Íslenzkir Annálar*, in *Sturlunga saga Including the Islendinga saga of lawman Sturla Thordsson and Other Works*, ed. G. Vigfusson, 2 vols. (Oxford, 1878), ii, 369 (s.a. 1223); *ES*, ii, 454–455.

44. *CRMI*, f. 43r.

45. *CRMI*, f. 44r.

46. *CRMI*, f. 44v.

47. *Chronicon de Lanercost*, ed. J. Stevenson (Edinburgh, 1839), 40 (misdated a year to 1228).

48. *The Saga of Hakon, and a Fragment of the Saga of Magnus, with Appendices*, trans. Sir G.W. Dasent. *Icelandic Sagas and Other Historical Documents Relating to the Settlements and Descents of the Northmen on the British Isles*, vol. 4 (London, 1894), 150–154; the modern edition is *Hákonar saga Hákonarsonar*, eds. Þ. Hauksson, S. Jakobsson, and T. Ulset, 2 vols. (Reykjavík, 2013), ii, 8–13. Discussion in McDonald, *Kingdom*, 88–91; Power, "Meeting in Norway," 44–46.

49. *CRMI*, f. 44v.

50. *Hákonar Saga*, 13 styled him *Svarti*, "The Black," Perhaps Mistaking *donn* for *dubh*: see B. Megaw, "Norseman and Native in the Kingdom of the Isles: A Re-assessment of the Manx Evidence," in P. Davey (ed.), *Man and Environment in the Isle of Man*, 2 vols. (Oxford, 1978), ii, 265–314 at 276–277.

51. Discussed further in McDonald, *Sea Kings*, chapter 6.
52. *CRMI*, f. 44v.
53. *CRMI*, f. 44v.
54. *Saga of Hakon* (trans. Dasent), 151–152.
55. Saga of Hakon (trans. Dassent), 154.
56. *CRMI*, f. 44v.
57. CRMI, f. 45r.
58. *CRMI*, f. 45v.
59. *CRMI*, f. 46r.
60. *CRMI*, f. 46v–47r; *Saga of Hakon* (trans. Dasent), 267–268.
61. *CRMI*, f. 47r.
62. *Sir Christopher Hatton's Book of Seals*, eds. L. Lewis and D.M. Stenton (Oxford, 1950), no. 428 (298–299, notes); *Monumenta de Insula Manniae, or a Collection of National Documents Relating to the Isle of Man*, ed. and trans. J.R. Oliver, 3 vols. (Douglas, 1860–1862), ii, 79. By the mid-thirteenth century the term *dominus* usually implied knightly status: see G. Duby, *The Chivalrous Society*, trans. C. Postan (Berkeley & Los Angeles, 1977), 75–77; D. Crouch, *The Image of Aristocracy in Britain, 1000–1300* (London & New York, 1992), 151. Ivar, his identity, and this episode are discussed further in McDonald, *Manx Kingship*, 88–91, 96–98.
63. *Foedera, conventiones, litterae, et cujuscunque generis acta publica, inter reges Angliae et alios quosvis imperatores, reges, pontifices, principes, vel communitates habita aut tractata*, ed. T. Rymer, 10 vols. (Hagae Comitis, 1739–1745), i, pt. ii, 12; Oliver, *Monumenta*, ii, 86 (misdated to 1255).
64. *CRMI*, f. 47r.
65. *CRMI*, f. 47v–48r.
66. *CRMI*, f. 48r.
67. *CRMI*, f. 48r.
68. *Calendar of Documents relating to Ireland, 1171–1307*, ed. H.S. Sweetman, 5 vols. (London, 1875–1886), I, no. 3206; *CRMI*, f. 49r.
69. *CRMI*, f. 49r.
70. McDonald, *Manx Kingship*, chapter 2; see also R.A. McDonald, "'Disharmony between Reginald and Olaf:' The Feud between the Sons of Godred II and Kin-Strife in the Kingdom of Man and the Isles, 1079–1265," in B.T. Hudson, (ed.), *Familia and Household in the Medieval Atlantic World* (Tempe, AZ, 2011), 155–176.
71. D. Carpenter, *The Struggle for Mastery. Britain 1066–1284* (London, 2003), 117; McDonald, *Manx Kingship*, 91.
72. Gerald of Wales, *The Journey Through Wales and the Description of Wales*, trans. with an intro by L. Thorpe (London, 1978), 261.

73. *Gesta regis Henrici secundi Benedicti abbatis*, ed. W. Stubbs, 2 vols. (London, 1867), i, 67–68; the authorship is now attributed to Roger of Howden: see A. Gransden, *Historical Writing in England c. 550 to c. 1307* (Ithaca, 1974), 222–230; see also J. Gillingham, "The Travels of Roger of Howden and His Views of the Irish, Scots and Welsh," *Anglo-Norman Studies* 20 (1997), 151–169.

74. *Orkneyinga Saga: The History of the Earls of Orkney*, trans. H. Pálsson and P. Edwards (London, 1981), chapters 111–112; see also R.A. McDonald, *Outlaws of Medieval Scotland: Challenges to the Canmore Kings, 1058–1266* (East Linton, 2003), 138–140.

75. J. Gillingham, "Killing and Mutilating Political Enemies in the British Isles from the Late Twelfth to the Early Fourteenth Century: A Comparative Study," in B. Smith (ed.), *Britain and Ireland 900–1300: Insular Responses to Medieval European Change* (Cambridge, 1999), 114–134 at 118; J. Gillingham, "Conquering the Barbarians: War and Chivalry in Britain and Ireland," in *The English in the Twelfth Century: Imperialism, National Identity, and Political Values* (Woodbridge, 2000), 41–58.

76. See, e.g., Gillingham, "1066 and the Introduction of Chivalry into England," in *The English in the Twelfth Century*, 209–232; M. Strickland, *War and Chivalry: The Conduct and Perception of War in England and Normandy 1066–1217* (Cambridge, 1996).

77. The whole topic is an interesting one that is pursued at greater length in McDonald, *Manx Kingship*, 214–218.

78. See e.g. R. Turvey, *The Welsh Princes, 1063–1283* (Harlow, 2002), 35.

79. "Magnúss saga berfoetts," in B. Adalbjarnarson (ed.), Snorri Sturluson, *Heimskringla*, 3 vols. (Reykjavík, 1941–1951), iii, 221. The term Northern Islands usually refers to Shetland and Orkney, but it is clear from the context that the northern Hebrides are meant here: see Anderson, *ES*, ii, 108, no. 6.

80. *Morkinskinna: The Earliest Icelandic Chronicle of the Norwegian Kings (1030–1157)*, trans. with introduction and notes by T.M. Andersson and K.E. Gade (Ithaca and London, 2000), 299–300: "The terror of kings [Magnús] captured the lord of North Uist at Skye and the Scots fled;" further discussion at 38–40 and 485. On Gísl see further K.E. Gade (ed.), *Poetry from the Kings' Sagas 2: From c. 1035 to c. 1300*, Skaldic Poetry of the Scandinavian Middle Ages 2 (Turnhout, 2009), 416–431. Andersson and Gade's rendering of *Ívistar* as 'North Uist' may be overly specific, as the Norse term appears to have been applied to North and South Uist as well as Benbecula: E. Beveridge, *North Uist: Its Archaeology and Topography with Notes Upon the Early History of the Outer Hebrides* (Edinburgh 1911; repr. 2001), 18–19. B.T. Hudson, *Viking Pirates and Christian Princes:*

Dynasty, Religion, and Empire in the North Atlantic (Oxford, 2005), 189 suggests that Uist might have been Lagman's residence.

81. *CRMI*, f. 36v.
82. *CRMI*, f. 37v–f. 38r.
83. McDonald, *Kingdom*, 56–57.
84. *CRMI*, f. 42v.
85. "Propaganda and Character Assassination": Stafford, "Portrayal of Royal Women," 146. It is worth noting that the reference to Rognvald's wife as *regina Insularum*, Queen of the Isles, is unique in the Chronicle and almost across the entire history of the dynasty. Ironically, perhaps, one of our last glimpses of the dynasty itself comes in the person of Mary of Argyll, the daughter of Ewen son of Duncan, Lord of Argyll (d.c. 1268), who married Magnus Olafsson, the last Manx king, sometime before his death in 1265. She outlived her Manx husband and went on to marry no fewer than three further times. She died in 1302 and was commonly described as "queen of Man" long after Magnus's death. Some basic information on her is collected at the People of Medieval Scotland Database: http://db.poms.ac.uk/record/person/7687; titles in *Edward I and the Throne of Scotland 1290–1296: An Edition of the Record Sources for the Great Cause*, ed. E.L.G. Stones and G.G. Simpson, 2 vols. (Oxford, 1978), ii, 125 ("Mary, queen of Man and countess of Strathearn" from 1291), and 367 ("Domina Mar[ia] regina de Man," appears, probably by mistake, among abbesses in a list of names in the Glasgow MS of those who swore fealty to Edward I in the summer of 1291). Further discussion is found in McDonald, *Sea Kings*, epilogue.
86. J. Beverley Smith, *Llywelyn ap Gruffudd: Prince of Wales* (Cardiff, 1998), 37–41, quote at 39. Coincidentally, there is a Manx connection here, since in the genealogies Llywelyn appears as a son of a woman named Rhunallt, said to have been a daughter of the king of Man: Smith, *Llywelyn ap Gruffudd*, 37–38; see also G. Broderick, "Irish and Welsh Strands in the Genealogy of Godred Crovan," *Journal of the Manx Museum* 8 (1980), 34, 35. Smith remarks that "no reliance may be placed upon [the Genealogies] in this respect": 38.
87. S.M. Johns, *Gender, Nation and Conquest in the High Middle Ages: Nest of Deheubarth* (Manchester, 2013), 5.
88. *CRMI*, f. 40v.
89. *The Statutes of the Isle of Man. Volume 1*, ed. J.F. Gill (London, 1883; repr. 1992), 55, 68.
90. *CRMI*, f. 40r.
91. B. Ó'Cuív, "A Poem in Praise of Raghnall, King of Man," *Éigse* 8 (1956–1957), 283–301, at 289, 293; there is also a translation in *The Triumph*

Tree: Scotland's Earliest Poetry AD 550–1350, ed. T.O. Clancy (Edinburgh, 1998), 236–241.

92. Ó'Cuív, 299, no. 8, cannot identify her, but states, "The name suggests that she was of Gaelic stock." This was the second most popular female name in later medieval Ireland: D. Ó Corráin and F. Maguire, *Gaelic Personal Names* (Dublin, 1981), 160.

93. *Calendar of Documents Relating to Scotland Preserved in Her Majesty's Public Record Office, London,* 5 vols: vols. 1–4, ed. J. Bain (Edinburgh, 1881–1888), vol. 5, eds. J.D. Galbraith and G.G. Simpson (Edinburgh, 1986), v, no. 9, 136.

94. B. Megaw, "Norseman and Native in the Kingdom of the Isles: A Re-assessment of the Manx Evidence," in P. Davey (ed.), *Man and Environment in the Isle of Man,* 2 vols. (Oxford, 1978), ii, 278, states emphatically that Rognvald was not the son of Godred and Finnguala.

95. I. Wood, "Kings, Kingdom and Consent," in P.H. Sawyer and I. Wood (eds.), *Early Medieval Kingship* (Leeds, 1977), 14.

96. B. Jaski, *Early Irish Kingship and Succession* (Dublin, 2000), 153.

97. Stafford, "Portrayal of Royal Women," 146.

BIBLIOGRAPHY

Beveridge, E. 1911. *North Uist: Its Archaeology and Topography with Notes Upon the Early History of the Outer Hebrides.* Edinburgh; repr. 2001.

Broderick, G. 1980. Irish and Welsh Strands in the Genealogy of Godred Crovan. *Journal of the Manx Museum* 8: 32–38.

Bull, M. 2005. *Thinking Medieval: An Introduction to the Study of the Middle Ages.* Basingstoke.

Calendar of Documents Relating to Ireland, 1171–1307. 1875–1886. Edited by H.S. Sweetman, 5 vols. London.

Calendar of Documents Relating to Scotland Preserved in Her Majesty's Public Record Office, London. 1986. Edited by J.D. Galbraith and G.G. Simpson, vol. 5. Edinburgh; Edited by J. Bain, 5 vols.: vols. 1–4. Edinburgh, 1881–1888.

Candon, A. 2006. Power, Politics and Polygamy: Women and Marriage in Late Pre-Norman Ireland. In *Ireland and Europe in the Twelfth Century: Reform and Renewal,* ed. D. Bracken and D. Ó Riain-Raedel, 106–127. Dublin.

Carpenter, D. 2003. *The Struggle for Mastery. Britain 1066–1284.* London.

Chronicon de Lanercost. 1839. Edited by J. Stevenson. Edinburgh.

Clarke, H.B. 2014. The Mother's Tale. In *Tales of Medieval Dublin,* ed. S. Booker and C.N. Peters, 52–62. Dublin.

Cronica Regum Mannie & Insularum. Chronicles of the Kings of Man and the Isles BL Cotton Julius A vii. 1995. Edited by G. Broderick, 2nd ed. Douglas; repr. 1996; 1st ed., 1979.

Crouch, D. 1992. *The Image of Aristocracy in Britain, 1000–1300*. London and New York.

Davies, R.R. 1980. The Status of Women and the Practice of Marriage in Late-Medieval Wales. In *The Welsh Law of Women*, ed. D. Jenkins and M. Owen, 93–114. Cardiff.

Duby, G. 1977. *The Chivalrous Society*. Translated by C. Postan. Berkeley and Los Angeles.

Duffy, S. 1995. The First Ulster Plantation: John de Courcy and the Men of Cumbria. In *Colony and Frontier in Medieval Ireland: Essays Presented to J.F. Lydon*, ed. T.B. Barry, R. Frame, and K. Simms, 1–28. London.

Early Sources of Scottish History, A.D. 500–1286. 1922. Edited and translated by A.O. Anderson, 2 vols. Edinburgh; repr. Stamford, 1990.

Edward I and the Throne of Scotland 1290–1296: An Edition of the Record Sources for the Great Cause. 1978. Edited by E.L.G. Stones and G.G. Simpson, 2 vols. Oxford.

Ferguson, P.C. 1997. *Medieval Papal Representatives in Scotland: Legates, Nuncios, and Judges-Delegate, 1125–1286*. Edinburgh.

Flanders, S. 2008. *De Courcy: Anglo-Normans in Ireland, England and France in the Eleventh and Twelfth Centuries*. Dublin.

Foedera, conventiones, litterae, et cujuscunque generis acta publica, inter reges Angliae et alios quosvis imperatores, reges, pontifices, principes, vel communitates habita aut tractata. 1739–1745. Edited by T. Rymer, 10 vols. Hagae Comitis.

Frame, R. 1990. *The Political Development of the British Isles, 1100–1400*. Oxford.

Gade, K.E., ed. 2009. *Poetry from the Kings' Sagas 2: From c. 1035 to c. 1300*, Skaldic Poetry of the Scandinavian Middle Ages 2. Turnhout.

Gerald of Wales. 1978. *The Journey Through Wales and the Description of Wales*. Translated with an introduction by L. Thorpe. London.

Gesta regis Henrici secundi Benedicti abbatis. 1867. Edited by W. Stubbs, 2 vols. London.

Gillingham, J. 1997. The Travels of Roger of Howden and His Views of the Irish, Scots and Welsh. *Anglo-Norman Studies* 20: 151–169.

———. 1999. Killing and Mutilating Political Enemies in the British Isles from the Late Twelfth to the Early Fourteenth Century: A Comparative Study. In *Britain and Ireland 900–1300: Insular Responses to Medieval European Change*, ed. B. Smith, 114–134. Cambridge.

———. 2000. *The English in the Twelfth Century: Imperialism, National Identity, and Political Values*. Woodbridge.

Giraldus Cambrensis (Gerald of Wales). 1978. *Expugnatio Hibernica. The Conquest of Ireland*. Edited and translated by A.B. Scott and F.X. Martin. Dublin.

Gransden, A. 1974. *Historical Writing in England c. 550–c. 1307*. Ithaca.

Hákonar saga Hákonarsonar. 2013. Edited by Þ. Hauksson, S. Jakobsson, and T. Ulset, 2 vols. Reykjavík.

Head, T. Hagiography. The Orb: The On-line Reference Book for Medieval Studies at http://www.hagiographysociety.org/wp-content/uploads/2013/03/Head_Hagiography.pdf

Highland Papers. 1914–1934. Edited by J.R.N. MacPhail, 4 vols. Edinburgh.

Hudson, B.T. 2005. *Viking Pirates and Christian Princes: Dynasty, Religion, and Empire in the North Atlantic.* Oxford.

Íslenzkir Annálar. 1878. In *Sturlunga Saga Including the Islendinga Saga of Lawman Sturla Thordsson and Other Works,* ed. G. Vigfusson, 2 vols. Oxford.

Jaski, B. 1996. Marriage Laws in Ireland and on the Continent in the Early Middle Ages. In *The Fragility of Her Sex'? Medieval Irish Women in Their European Context,* ed. C. Meek and K. Simms, 16–42. Dublin.

———. 2000. *Early Irish Kingship and Succession.* Dublin.

Jochens, J. 1987. The Politics of Reproduction: Medieval Norwegian Kingship. *American Historical Review* 92: 327–349.

Johns, Susan M. 2013. *Gender, Nation and Conquest in the High Middle Ages: Nest of Deheubarth.* Manchester.

The Letters of Lanfranc Archbishop of Canterbury. 1979. Edited and translated by H. Clover and M. Gibson. Oxford.

Martin, F.X. 1987. John, Lord of Ireland, 1185–1216. In *New History of Ireland Volume 2: Medieval Ireland, 1169–1534,* ed. A. Cosgrove, 127–155. Oxford.

McDonald, R.A. 1995. Matrimonial Politics and Core-Periphery Interactions in Twelfth- and Early Thirteenth-Century Scotland. *Journal of Medieval History* 21: 227–247.

———. 1997. *The Kingdom of the Isles: Scotland's Western Seaboard, c. 1100–c. 1336.* East Linton.

———. 2003a. Old and New in the Far North: Ferchar Maccintsacairt and the Early Earls of Ross, c.1200–74. In *The Exercise of Power in Medieval Scotland, c. 1200–1500,* ed. S. Boardman and A. Ross, 23–45. Dublin.

———. 2003b. *Outlaws of Medieval Scotland: Challenges to the Canmore Kings, 1058–1266.* East Linton.

———. 2007. *Manx Kingship in its Irish Sea Setting 1187–1229: King Rögnvaldr and the Crovan Dynasty.* Dublin.

———. 2011. 'Disharmony between Reginald and Olaf:' The Feud between the Sons of Godred II and Kin-Strife in the Kingdom of Man and the Isles, 1079–1265. In *Familia and Household in the Medieval Atlantic World,* ed. B.T. Hudson, 155–176. Tempe, AZ.

———. 2019. *The Sea Kings: The Late Norse Kingdoms of Man and the Isles, 1066–1275.* Edinburgh.

Megaw, B.R.S. 1978. Norseman and Native in the Kingdom of the Isles: A Re-assessment of the Manx Evidence. In *Man and Environment in the Isle of Man,* ed. P.J. Davey, vol. ii, 265–314. Oxford.

Monumenta de Insula Manniae, or a Collection of National Documents Relating to the Isle of Man. 1860–1862. Edited and translated by J.R. Oliver, 3 vols. Douglas.

Morkinskinna: The Earliest Icelandic Chronicle of the Norwegian Kings (1030–1157). 2000. Translated with introduction and notes by T.M. Andersson and K.E. Gade. Ithaca and London.

Ó Corráin, D. 1978. Women in Early Irish Society. In *Women in Irish Society: The Historical Dimension,* ed. M. MacCurtain and D. Ó Corráin, 1–13. Dublin.

———. 1985. Marriage in Early Ireland. In *Marriage in Ireland,* ed. A. Cosgrove, 5–24. Dublin.

Ó Corráin, D., and F. Maguire. 1981. *Gaelic Personal Names.* Dublin.

Ó Cróinín, D. 1995. *Early Medieval Ireland, 400–1200.* London.

Ó'Cuív, B. 1956–1957. A Poem in Praise of Raghnall, King of Man. *Éigse* 8: 283–301.

Oram, R., and P. Adderley. 2010. Innse Gall: Culture and Environment on a Norse Frontier in the Western Isles. In *The Norwegian Domination and the Norse World c.1100–c.1400,* ed. S. Imsen, 125–148. Trondheim.

Orkneyinga Saga: The History of the Earls of Orkney. 1981. Translated by H. Pálsson and P. Edwards. London.

Power, R. 2005. Meeting in Norway: Norse-Gaelic Relations in the kingdom of Man and the Isles, 1090–1270. *Saga Book* 29: 5–66.

Pryce, H. 1993. *Native Law and the Church in Medieval Wales.* Oxford.

Royal Commission on Ancient and Historical Monuments and Constructions of Scotland. 1928. *Ninth Report, With Inventory of Monuments and Constructions in the Outer Hebrides, Skye and the Small Isles.* Edinburgh.

The Saga of Hakon, and a Fragment of the Saga of Magnus, with Appendices. 1894. Translated by Sir G.W. Dasent. *Icelandic Sagas and Other Historical Documents Relating to the Settlements and Descents of the Northmen on the British Isles,* vol. 4. London.

Sellar, W.D.H. 1978–1980. Marriage, Divorce and Concubinage in Gaelic Scotland. *Transactions of the Gaelic Society of Inverness* 51: 464–493.

———. 1997–1998. The Ancestry of the MacLeods Reconsidered. *Transactions of the Gaelic Society of Inverness* 60: 233–258.

Sharples, N., and R. Smith. 2009. Norse Settlement in the Western Isles. In *Scandinavian Scotland—Twenty Years After: The Proceedings of a Day Conference held on 19 February 2007,* ed. A. Woolf, 103–130. St. Andrews.

Sir Christopher Hatton's Book of Seals. 1950. Edited by L. Lewis and D.M. Stenton. Oxford.

Small, A. 1976. Norse Settlement in Skye. In *Les Vikings et leur civilization. Problèmes actuels,* ed. R. Boyer, 29–37. Paris.

Smith, J. 1998. Beverley. In *Llywelyn ap Gruffudd: Prince of Wales.* Cardiff.

Stafford, P. 1983. *Queens, Concubines and Dowagers: The King's Wife in the Early Middle Ages.* London.

————. 1996. The Portrayal of Royal Women in England, Mid-tenth to Mid-twelfth Centuries. In *Medieval Queenship*, ed. J.C. Parsons, 143–167. New York.

The Statutes of the Isle of Man. Volume 1. 1883. Edited by J.F. Gill. London; repr. 1992.

Strickland, M. 1996. *War and Chivalry: The Conduct and Perception of War in England and Normandy 1066–1217.* Cambridge.

Sturluson, Snorri. 1941–1951. *Heimskringla.* Edited by B. Adalbjarnarson, 3 vols. Reykjavík.

Thomas, S. 2014. From Cathedral of the Isles to Obscurity—The Archaeology and History of Skeabost Island, Snizort. *Proceedings of the Society of Antiquaries of Scotland* 144: 245–264.

The Triumph Tree: Scotland's Earliest Poetry AD 550–1350. 1998. Edited by T.O. Clancy. Edinburgh.

Turvey, R. 2002. *The Welsh Princes, 1063–1283.* Harlow.

Wood, I. 1977. Kings, Kingdom and Consent. In *Early Medieval Kingship*, ed. P.H. Sawyer and I. Wood, 6–29. Leeds.

Woolf, A. 2004. The Age of Sea-Kings: 900–1300. In *The Argyll Book*, ed. D. Omand, 94–109. Edinburgh.

WEBSITES

People of Medieval Scotland Database: http://db.poms.ac.uk/record/person/7687

CHAPTER 7

Conclusion: Kings, Usurpers, Concubines, and Chroniclers

Abstract Although the Manx sea kings naturally constitute the focus of the *Chronicles of the Kings of Man and the Isles*, drilling more deeply into the text reveals that not all members of the dynasty receive neutral treatment. From 1187 onwards the text can be read as an account of the struggle between two rival branches of the kindred, represented by the brothers Rognvald and Olaf Godredsson. The production of the text in the reign of Magnus Olafsson (d. 1265), which witnessed the ultimate triumph of the line of Olaf, suggests that the *Chronicles* played a role in legitimizing his kingship. One of the principal messages embedded within the text, particularly within its account of the feud between the two brothers, is that of female responsibility for the feuding that frequently plagued the kingdom.

Keywords *Chronicles of the Kings of Man and the Isles* • Crovan kings • Kingdom of Man and the Isles • Kingship • Kin-feud • Magnus Olafsson

The mid-thirteenth-century text known as the *Chronicles of the Kings of Man and the Isles* is the single most important piece of evidence historians possess for unravelling the relatively obscure history of the Kingdom of Man and the Isles under the Crovan kings from the late eleventh to the late thirteenth centuries. Although these rulers and their exploits appear in

© The Author(s) 2019

R. A. McDonald, *Kings, Usurpers, and Concubines in the* Chronicles of the Kings of Man and the Isles,
https://doi.org/10.1007/978-3-030-22026-6_7

a variety of other medieval documents ranging from Icelandic sagas to Scottish charters, English administrative records, and papal correspondence, the *Chronicles* provide an unmatched level of unique information. Without them, our knowledge of the period would be greatly diminished, and much of the age of the sea kings in Man and the Isles would remain a virtual blank.

Historians have, accordingly, utilized the *Chronicles* as a crucial piece of evidence for a wide range of investigations relating to political, social, economic, cultural, and religious history, never more so than in the past 20 years or so.[1] But while modern historians may utilize texts in a variety of ways, the original purpose of the text must always be borne in mind. Even a cursory reading of the *Chronicles* will suggest that one of its principal purposes is to relate the deeds of the Manx sea kings descended from Godred Crovan. These kings are clearly the focus of the text, which is interested in their doings, including their relations with neighbouring powers, their marriages, their religious patronage, and much else. They are, if we like, the "heroes" of the text, and their presentation in this guise underlined by the depiction of dynastic rivals, like Somerled and his descendants, or those who would take over the kingdom, like the Scottish kings, in a negative manner in the text.

However, drilling more deeply into the fabric of the *Chronicles* reveals that not all members of the Manx royal dynasty receive equal treatment. Although there had been fractures and rivalries within the dynasty before the reign of King Godred Olafsson, the death of this king in 1187 and the subsequent rivalry between his sons Rognvald and Olaf and their descendants for the kingship brought a new level of competition and fractiousness to the kingdom that endured through the remaining decades of the transmarine realm. The *Chronicles* pay particular attention to this competition, but, perhaps more importantly, the text is not neutral in its treatment of two lines of kings descended from the brothers. Reaching back to the death of King Godred in 1187 and the succession of King Rognvald, and throughout its account of the thirteenth-century kings, the *Chronicles* treats the line of King Rognvald as illegitimate and that of King Olaf as legitimate—as, for instance, in its account of the events of 1249–1250, when it says, "Then Harald, son of Godred Don, usurped the title and dignity of king in Man for himself."[2]

The Manx chronicle, then, represents more than just a straightforward narrative of the kings in Man and the Isles descended from Godred Crovan, although it can certainly be read this way. From 1187 onwards, however, it can also be read as an account of the struggle between two rival branches of the kindred sprung from Godred Olafsson, the grandson of the dynasty's founder. Not only this, but its production in the reign of Magnus Olafsson (d. 1265), which witnessed the ultimate triumph of the line of Olaf over the line of Rognvald, suggests that the *Chronicles* in fact played a role in legitimizing the kingship of Magnus and his line, perhaps in the face of ongoing opposition—and, ironically, only about a decade before the death of Magnus and the Scottish takeover of the island marked the end of the kingdom once and for all.[3] The Manx chronicle is therefore a product of, as well as a narrative of, the kin-strife within the Crovan dynasty.[4]

Moreover, I suggest that one of the principal messages embedded within the text is that of female responsibility for the factionalism and feuding that frequently plagued the Kingdom of Man and the Isles. This message is evident with the chronicler's condemnation of the practice of concubinage. We have noted, for instance, the statement that the marriage of one of Olaf Godredsson's daughters by a concubine to Somerled of Argyll was "the cause of the collapse of the entire kingdom of the Isles," and the characterization of the desire of King Rognvald's wife to eliminate her husband's brother around 1223 as her "wicked wish." More subtly, and, therefore, perhaps more tellingly, the message is conveyed through the chronicler's clever device of withholding the name of King Rognvald's wife, styled only "Queen of the Isles," when it is very difficult indeed to believe that her name was not known to the author. This therefore appears as propaganda and character assassination[5] on a grand scale. In short, it would appear that the principal compiler of the Manx chronicle shared the view of the near-contemporary churchman and scholar Giraldus Cambrensis (Gerald of Wales, d.c. 1223), who famously remarked in his *Expugnatio Hibernica* of c. 1189 that: "Almost all the world's most notable catastrophes have been caused by women."[6]

Notes

1. As amply demonstrated by many of the contributions to S. Duffy and H. Mytum (eds.), *A New History of the Isle of Man, Volume III. The Medieval Period 1000–1406* (Liverpool, 2015).
2. *CRMI*, f. 47v.
3. The point is also made by B. Williams, "Chronicles of the Kings of Man and the Isles," in S. Duffy and H. Mytum (eds.), *A New History of the Isle of*

Man, Volume III. The Medieval Period 1000–1406 (Liverpool, 2015), 305–326. Gransden notes the role for chronicles as potential vessels of propaganda: A. Gransden, "The Chronicles of Medieval England and Scotland," in *Legends, Traditions and History in Medieval England* (London and Rio Grande, 1992), 219–220.

4. R.A. McDonald, *Manx Kingship in Its Irish Sea Setting 1187–1229: King Rögnvaldr and the Crovan Dynasty* (Dublin, 2007), 100.

5. P. Stafford, "The Portrayal of Royal Women in England, Mid-tenth to Mid-twelfth Centuries," in J.C. Parsons (ed.), *Medieval Queenship* (New York, 1996), 145–146.

6. Giraldus Cambrensis (Gerald of Wales). *Expugnatio Hibernica. The Conquest of Ireland*, ed. and trans. A.B. Scott and F.X. Martin (Dublin, 1978), 24–25.

BIBLIOGRAPHY

Duffy, S., and H. Mytum, eds. 2015. *A New History of the Isle of Man, Volume III. The Medieval Period 1000–1406*. Liverpool.

Giraldus Cambrensis (Gerald of Wales). 1978. *Expugnatio Hibernica. The Conquest of Ireland*. Edited and translated by A.B. Scott and F.X. Martin. Dublin.

Gransden, A. 1992. The Chronicles of Medieval England and Scotland. In *Legends, Traditions and History in Medieval England*, 199–238. London and Rio Grande.

McDonald, R.A. 2007. *Manx Kingship in its Irish Sea Setting 1187–1229: King Rögnvaldr and the Crovan Dynasty*. Dublin.

Stafford, P. 1996. The Portrayal of Royal Women in England, Mid-tenth to Mid-twelfth Centuries. In *Medieval Queenship*, ed. J.C. Parsons, 143–167. New York.

Williams, B. 2015. Chronicles of the Kings of Man and the Isles. In *A New History of the Isle of Man, Volume III. The Medieval Period 1000–1406*, ed. S. Duffy and H. Mytum, 305–326. Liverpool.

Index[1]

---

[1] Note: Page numbers followed by 'n' refer to notes.

© The Author(s) 2019
R. A. McDonald, *Kings, Usurpers, and Concubines in the* Chronicles of the Kings of Man and the Isles,
https://doi.org/10.1007/978-3-030-22026-6

95

Printed by Printforce, the Netherlands